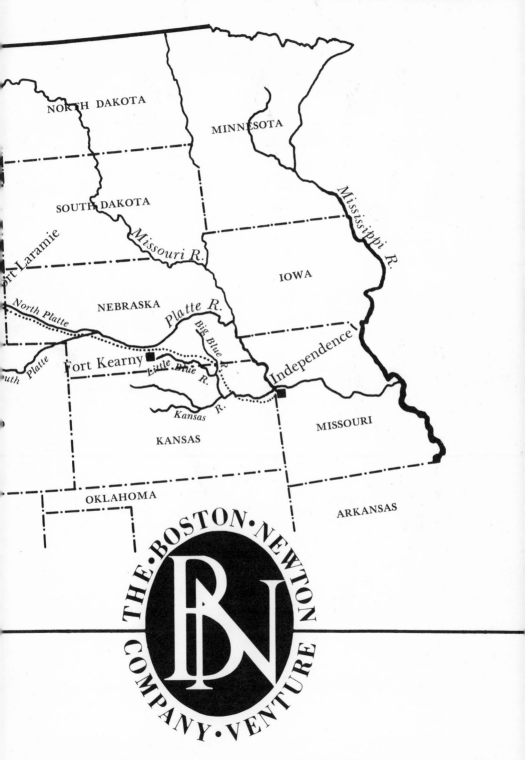

NORTH DAKOTA

MINNESOTA

SOUTH DAKOTA

Missouri R.

Mississippi R.

Fort Laramie

IOWA

North Platte

NEBRASKA

Platte R.

Big Blue R.

Independence

South Platte

Fort Kearny

Little Blue R.

Kansas R.

MISSOURI

KANSAS

OKLAHOMA

ARKANSAS

THE·BOSTON·NEWTON
COMPANY·VENTURE

THE
BOSTON-NEWTON
COMPANY VENTURE

From Massachusetts to California in 1849

Jessie Gould Hannon

UNIVERSITY OF NEBRASKA PRESS · LINCOLN

Manufactured in the United States of America

To

the descendants

of the men of the Boston-Newton Joint Stock Association

whose encouragement

and assistance in collecting material

made this volume possible

CONTENTS

A picture section follows page 122

LIST OF MAPS

PREFACE

This volume brings together companion diaries kept by Charles Gould and David Jackson Staples, members of the Boston-Newton Joint Stock Association, during the company's overland journey from Boston to Sutter's Fort in the spring and summer of 1849. The journal of my grandfather, Charles Gould, has never before appeared in print; the Staples journal was published in the *California Historical Society Quarterly* in 1943, edited by Harold F. Taggart, but has not previously been collected.

Although the literature of the American West is rich in accounts of the epic of the forty-niners, it seems to me that this day-to-day narrative of the Boston-Newton company venture holds a special place for several reasons. First, the pairing of diaries by two men of quite different temperaments gives us an unusual double perspective. Moreover, I have been able to supplement the diaries with letters and recollections of other members of the party, and from family records, all of which help to fill in and round out the picture. Second, the members of the Boston-Newton company do not exist in a vacuum: in nearly all cases, we know not only where they came from and what kind of men they were, but what happened to them after they reached the Land of Gold. Third, as Harold F. Taggart has pointed out, the best known accounts of the migration of the forty-niners concern those expeditions which experienced great difficulties. But, as he notes, "many groups came through after months of hardships and dogged persistence and entered California with no fanfare," and the Boston-Newton venture "probably typifies the experiences of the great majority." Fourth, and not least important, the members embody those qualities of the American character which made our people peculiarly suited for pioneering —courage and steadfastness, ingenuity and optimism, loyalty and the ability to work together for the common good.

The men of the Boston-Newton company were a homogeneous group—all New Englanders, mostly from the Boston-Newton area, several of them related. They were not flamboyant, hard-bitten adventurers, skilled in the frontier arts: they were average citizens—if any pioneer may be so described—sober and God-fearing family men, not looking for excitement, seeking solely to better themselves. No doubt these factors, plus careful planning and preparation, explain why the Boston-Newton company is credited with being the only organized group of forty-niners to reach California without a change of officers en route. They also explain why the twin accounts of the journey are low in key—rich in homely details and devoid of exclamation points, with the drama largely implicit. Yet both diarists were perceptive men, and one of the great delights in reading their narratives is that we see through their eyes the wonders of that great stretch of land from the Missouri to the Western Ocean when everything was new, before civilization had put its mark on it. Charles Gould and David Staples and their companions did not fight any Indians, but they did stop to pick flowers—indeed, some of these blossoms are still to be seen, pressed between the pages of Charles's journal.

Keeping a diary up to date on the trail was not an easy thing to do. Sometimes the account was started in the morning and completed in the evening. Wagons and riders were stretched out on the road, so that the men in the rear did not see or hear what was happening half a mile or more up front, and vice versa. In camp the men often discussed the happenings of the day and a variety of opinions emerged on what had taken place. In the end, the diarist gave his personal version of events. Yet there are surprisingly few discrepancies in the Gould and Staples accounts;

rather, they dovetail, one account supplementing the other as each man noted down what had most impressed him during the day. After the opening chapters, in which I have aimed to supply background information and to introduce the members of the company, the story of the journey is told almost entirely by the two diarists. The concluding chapter, about the disbanding of the company, and the Epilogue are derived from other primary materials, as described in the Note on Sources.

While it is my hope that this book will be of service to scholars, and for this reason I have tried to make the documentation complete, my original purpose was to put together a narrative that could be read with enjoyment by the nonspecialist and I have not been concerned to reproduce exactly the style and orthography of the two journals. I have supplied capitals and punctuation where it seemed to me they would be helpful to the reader, and I have made consistent the spelling of some place names, chiefly the names of states and of eastern cities. Also in the interest of easier reading, I had substituted *and* for *&* (though I have let *&c.—* for *et cetera*—stand) and *company* for *co.* when it refers to the Boston-Newton company or other groups crossing the plains; and I have followed modern usage in closing up such forms to *today* and *tonight* (for *to-day* and *to-night*), *everything* and *sometimes* (*every thing* and *some times*). Otherwise the original grammar and spelling has been left unaltered—and the spelling frequently *is* original, especially of words pertaining to the western country. Thus, the reader sometimes will find variant spellings of a word such as *prairie* in a single diary entry. The same editorial principles have been applied to the letters from George Winslow and Brackett Lord which appear in Chapters 5 and 6, but other quoted material is given exactly as it appears in the source from which I took it.

In Chapters 4 and 5, describing the journey from Boston to Independence and the stay at Camp Grove, portions of the diary entries which duplicated details have been omitted. These omissions are indicated by suspension points (. . .). In the following chapters the text of both diaries is given in full. Words that I have supplied are enclosed in brackets. In the few cases where a word was illegible and I have had to guess at it, the word is enclosed in brackets with a question mark. I have given the diary dates in consistent form.

Elsewhere in this book I have formally acknowledged my debt to the many people and agencies whose help has been indispensable in carrying through this project. But I would like to say here a special word of thanks to the Bancroft Library, where I did most of my research; to the Nebraska State Historical Society, which made available many relevant materials; to the Minnesota Historical Society and George A. Rossman for allowing me to use the original Gould journal; and to the *California State Historical Society Quarterly* and Harold F. Taggart for permission to use the Staples journal as edited by Mr. Taggart, which was the text I followed except in the respects specified above.

THE BOSTON-NEWTON COMPANY VENTURE

Take the Bible in one hand and your
New England civilization in the other
and make your mark on that country.

EDWARD EVERETT

CHAPTER 1

Gold Fever

When President James K. Polk, in his farewell message to Congress on December 5, 1848, referred in the most enthusiastic terms to goldmining prospects in California, he gave official confirmation to rumors which had been seeping eastward for the past ten months. The story of the California gold rush actually begins on January 24, 1848, when James W. Marshall, who was supervising the construction of a sawmill on the Coloma River, noticed a number of bright, brass-colored particles in the tailrace. Suspecting that they might be gold, he at once hastened to report the find to his partner, Johann Augustus Sutter, at Sutter's Fort, at the junction of the Sacramento and American rivers, some fifty-four miles distant.[1]

Sutter himself has described what happened when Marshall reached the fort.

---

[1] A German emigrant of Swiss parentage, Sutter (1803–1880) came to America in 1834 and settled in California in 1839. In 1841, the year that he built Sutter's Fort, he received from the Spanish governor a grant of 141,000 acres in the Sacramento Valley. He acquired cattle and horses, sowed grain and planted vineyards, and built barns, granaries, warehouses, a tannery, a grist mill, and a winery. By all odds, Sutter was the most widely known and influential of the early settlers in this region.

It was a rainy afternoon when Mr. Marshall arrived at my office in the Fort, very wet. I was somewhat surprised to see him, as he was down a few days previous. He told me then that he had some important and interesting news that he wished to communicate secretly to me, and wished me to go with him to a place where we should not be disturbed, and where no listeners could come and hear what we had to say. I went with him to my private room; he requested me to lock the door. I complied, but told him at the same time, there was nobody in the house except the clerk, who was in his office in a different part of the house. After requesting something of me which my servant brought and then left the room, I forgot to lock the door, and it happened that the door was opened by the clerk just at the moment when Marshall took a rag from his pocket, showing me the yellow metal. He had about two ounces of it; but how quick Mr. Marshall put the yellow metal in his pocket again can hardly be described.

The clerk came to see me on business, and excused himself for interrupting me. As soon as he had left, I was told, "Now lock the door: didn't I tell you we might have listeners?" I told him he need not fear that; but I could hardly convince him he need not be suspicious. Then Mr. Marshall began to show me this metal, which consisted of small pieces and specimens, some of them worth a few dollars. . . . He had expressed his opinion to the laborers at the mill, that this might be gold; but some of them were laughing at him . . . and could not believe such a thing.[2]

---

[2] Lawson B. Patterson, *Twelve Years in the Mines of California* (Cambridge, 1862), quoted in Robert W. Richmond and Robert W. Mardock, eds., *A Nation Moving West: Readings in the History of the American Frontier* (Lincoln: University of Nebraska Press, 1966), p. 195. The quotation following is from the same source, pp. 195–196.

2

Not until the two men had made some tests was Sutter convinced that the bright-colored particles were gold. Having looked up an article in the encyclopedia which gave a formula for determing the specific gravity of old metals and rules for finding the quantity of each, they had to hunt over the whole fort to find three dollars and a half in silver to use in the computation which proved that Marshall's find was "pure stuff." Sutter said that he

> thought a good deal during the night about the consequences that might follow such a discovery, and left the next morning for Coloma in a heavy rain. About half way on the road I saw at a distance a human being crawling out from the brush-wood. When I came nearer I found it was Marshall, very wet. He had been to Coloma, took his other horse, and had returned to meet me. We rode to the new El Dorado, and in the afternoon, the weather clearing up, made a prospecting promenade. The next morning we went to the tail-race of the mill, through which the water was running during the night, to clean out the gravel which had been made loose, for the purpose of widening the race. After the water was out we went in and searched for gold. This was done every morning. Small pieces of gold could be seen remaining on the bottom of the clean washed bed rock. I went into the race and picked up several pieces; several of the laborers gave me some which they had picked up, and from Marshall I received a part. I have had a heavy ring made of this gold, with my family's coat of arms engraved on the outside, and on the inside is engraved, *"The first gold discovered in January, 1848."*

Sutter and Marshall gave the workmen at the mill permission to try their luck at gold prospecting and all were agreed that the news should be kept quiet at least until the mill was finished. But it could hardly be hoped that such a sensational discovery, known to so many, could be kept secret, and Sutter himself, when he returned to the fort, kept dropping portentous hints about something earthshaking that had happened at Coloma. Sutter's employees at the fort from the cook to the clerk deserted their jobs to hunt gold, and before many weeks had passed, strangers began to appear at the mill armed with pans and shovels and picks. By the end of May, three-fourths of the men in San Francisco had headed inland to the gold fields; sailors deserted vessels in the harbor; and businesses closed their doors. Both of the city's newspapers had to stop publishing, and on May 29, the editor of the *Californian* recorded in the paper's last issue:

> The whole country from San Francisco to Los Angeles, and from the seashore to the base of the Sierra Nevada resounds to the sordid cry of gold! gold!! gold!!! while the field is left half planted, the house half built, and everything neglected but the manufacture of shovels and pickaxes.

On June 1, Thomas O. Larkin, U.S. Naval Agent at Monterey, wrote to Secretary of State James Buchanan in Washington:

> I have to report to the State Department one of the most astonishing excitements and state of affairs now existing in this country, that, perhaps, has ever been brought to the notice of the government. On the American fork of the Sacramento and Feather river, another branch of the same, and the adjoining lands, there has been, within the present year, discovered a placer, a vast tract of land containing gold, in small particles. This gold, thus far, has been taken on the bank of the river, from the surface to eighteen inches in depth, and is supposed deeper, and to extend over the country. On account of the inconvenience of washing, the people have, to this time, only gathered the metal on the banks, which is done simply with a shovel, filling a shallow dish, bowl, basket, or tin pan with a quantity of black sand, similar to the class used on paper, and washing out the sand by movement of the vessel. It is now two or three weeks since the men employed in these washings have appeared in

4

this town [San Francisco] with gold, to exchange for merchandise and provisions. I presume near twenty thousand dollars . . . of this gold has, as yet, been so exchanged. . . . I have seen the written statement of the work of one man for sixteen days, which averaged twenty-five dollars ($25) per day; others have, with a shovel and pan, or wooden bowl, washed out ten to even fifty dollars in a day. There are now some men yet washing, who have five hundred to one thousand dollars. As they have to stand two feet deep in the river, they work but a few hours in the day, and not every day in the week. . . . I am confident that this town has one-half of its tenements empty, locked up with the furniture. The owners—storekeepers, lawyers, mechanics, and laborers— all gone to the Sacramento with their families. Small parties, of five to fifteen men, have sent to this town and offered cooks ten to fifteen dollars per day for a few weeks. Mechanics and teamsters, earning the year past five to eight dollars per day, have struck and gone. Several United States volunteers have deserted. United States barque Anita, belonging to the army, now at anchor here, has but six men. . . . Common spades and shovels, one month ago worth one dollar, will now bring ten dollars at the gold regions. I am informed fifty dollars has been offered for one. Should this gold continue as represented, this town, and others, will be depopulated. Clerks' wages have rose from six hundred to one thousand dollars per annum, and board; cooks', twenty-five to thirty dollars per month. This sum will not be an inducement a month longer, unless the fever and ague appears among the washers. The "Californian," printed here, stopped this week. The "Star" newspaper office . . . has but one man left. A merchant, lately from China, has even lost his China servants. Should the excitement continue through this year, and the whale-ships visit San Francisco, I think they will lose most all their crews. . . . I have seen several pounds of this gold, and consider it very pure, worth, in New York,

5

seventeen to eighteen dollars per ounce. Fourteen to sixteen dollars, in merchandise, is paid for it here. What good or bad effect this gold region will have on California, I cannot foretell. It may end this year; but I am informed that it will continue many years. . . .[3]

Larkin's letter arrived in Washington in September via Cape Horn, but Lieutenant Edward F. Beale, United States Navy, who reached the capital on September 16 with dispatches from Commodore Jones, Commander of the Pacific Squadron, is credited by some authorities with bringing eastward the first "authentic" news of the discovery, in a trip made across Mexico.[4] At any rate on September 18 the New York *Herald* reported news of the great strike. The Boston *Herald* reprinted the item a day later, and by September 24 the story had reached St. Louis, where the *Weekly Item* observed that if the account was even half correct, there would soon be an increased tide of emigration flowing into California. "[Lieutenant Beale's] report of the extent and richness of the mines," declared the *Item*, "appears to point out our newly acquired possessions on the shores of the Pacific[5] as the no mistake El Dorado."

Already the gold fever was spreading, and after President Polk's message to Congress it reached epidemic proportions. On December 11, six days after the President's speech, the New York *Herald* stated "the gold fever is at its height. It is a leading topic of conversation in streets and markets." On the following day, the Boston *Daily Advertiser* noted that "the disease rages in

[3] *House Executive Document 1*, 30th Congress, 2d Session, quoted in Richmond and Mardock, *A Nation Moving West*, pp. 196–197.

[4] See Milo M. Quaife, ed., *Kit Carson's Autobiography* (Lincoln: University of Nebraska Press, 1966), p. 123, *n.* 108.

[5] Following the Mexican War of 1846, Mexico, by the terms of the Treaty of Guadalupe Hidalgo, ceded to the United States the area including the present states of California, Nevada, Utah, and the greater portions of Arizona and New Mexico. The treaty was signed just nine days after the discovery of gold at Sutter's Mill.

this city," and on December 24 the Pittsburgh *Daily Morning Post* chimed in:

> Ho for California! The accumulating evidences of the great mineral wealth of California are stirring up adventurous spirits in every section of the Union and preparing the way for an immense immigration between this period and the advance of Summer. Our exchanges from every quarter contain notices of the prevalence of the "gold fever" and of individuals and companies preparing to leave.

Some of these "notices" took the form of advertisements like the following which appeared in the New York *Tribune* under the heading CALIFORNIA COMPANIES.[6]

> A small select party to consist of not more than 25 members, is about forming to go by fast sailing vessel to proceed to the Sacramento River, with the necessary outfit for two years. $500–$1,000 each. Pizarro Association.

> A meeting of the New York Overland Mutual Protection Association for California will be held this evening, Feb. 3, 1849, at Dunlap's Hotel. A person will be in attendance during the day to give all necessary information as regards the route.

> A select party of 25 or 30 professional and mercantile gentlemen will start in a few weeks for San Francisco by a route combining celerity, economy & comfort in a higher degree than any usually proposed. A few vacancies remain which they will fill with gentlemen of the above character. Address "Cortez" at this office giving real names and reference.

[6] The first advertisement appeared on January 19, 1849; the other two on February 3, 1849.

All during the winter of 1848–1849 in cities and towns and hamlets throughout the eastern states California gold was the one great topic of conversation. For many men, it was not a question of whether they were going, but whom they would go with, how soon they could get started, and what route they would take. Frequently, friends and neighbors would form a California company, all contributing a certain sum for equipment and pledging themselves to stand by one another and render mutual aid on the journey. One such organization was the Boston-Newton Joint Stock Association.

CHAPTER 2

The Organization of the Boston-Newton Company

The founders and organizers of the Boston-Newton company were four young men who had first met eight years before, in 1841, on the morning that they applied for an apprenticeship course at the Petee Iron Works in Newton Upper Falls, Massachusetts. At this time three of the men—Charles Gould, David Staples, and George Winslow—were seventeen years old; the fourth, Brackett Lord, was twenty-one.[1] The exact date when they conceived the idea of the venture is not known, but undoubtedly it was toward the end of 1848 or early in 1849.

Although the story of the Boston-Newton company is the story of a group rather than of individuals, I will begin this account by introducing the reader to the two men who left a record of it: Charles Gould and David Staples. This is not to suggest that they played a more prominent role than other members of the company, but by virtue of the fact that they wrote the journals it is inevitable that they occupy the foreground. I should

---

[1] In 1911, when Charles Gould described the first meeting of the future founders of the company to George E. Hansen of Fairbury, Nebraska, he said that they were all seventeen. However, Brackett Lord was born on January 4, 1819.

add that if in this and subsequent chapters I seem to dwell on a half-dozen members of the company and slight the others, this is a matter of necessity rather than choice—they are the ones about whom the most information is available. I am aware too that it is not easy to sort out and keep straight twenty-five different men, and though this difficulty cannot be completely overcome, I believe that as the narrative progresses most of the members of the party emerge as distinct personalities.

Charles Gould's father, John Allen Gould, was born in 1795 at Milton, Massachusetts, the son of Captain Abraham Gould, a veteran of the Revolutionary War, and Rachel Horton Gould.[2] After Captain Gould's death, when John was ten or eleven, he was apprenticed to learn the carpenter's trade with Benjamin W. Glover at Quincy; and when he was fourteen he took further apprentice work with Samuel Allen of Walpole, completing it when he was twenty-one years of age. While at Walpole, he became acquainted with Rebecca Gay, daughter of Calvin Gay and Joanna Kingsbury Gay, whom he married on May 29, 1810. Gould joined the militia at Walpole and in 1812 was elected an ensign in the company, which was called out twice in the defense of Boston during the War of 1812. After the war, Major Gould— he had become a major in 1818—took on local responsibilities, serving as selectman, assessor, and collector of taxes, was administrator of estates and farmer of Walpole.

On April 3, 1824, Major Gould recorded in his journal: "Charles, my third son and fourth child, was born." The two older boys were John Allen, born in 1816, and George, born in 1820; Margaret, the Goulds' daughter, was born in 1829. Because of his own unhappy experiences as a result of being apprenticed at a tender age, Major Gould was determined that his sons, while

[2] Information about Major Gould and about Charles Gould's early life from the John Allen Gould Journal, now in the possession of Gardner Gould, Newtonville, Massachusetts. See also A Note on Sources.

they were growing up, would not be under the supervision of anyone other than their own parents and a schoolmaster he had chosen for them.

Charles began attending a private school on his fourth birthday. Besides mastering the three R's at school, at home he learned how to make wooden articles, such as miniature pieces of furniture, and how to weave cloth not only for the family but also to be sold. "Earn and save" was the motto the Major instilled in his sons, and as he was a firm believer in buying bonds, their first earnings were saved for this purpose. (An 1835 letter from George to John reads: "It is the same old story, Father is buying another bond.") Until they were twenty-one, each of the boys had to contribute toward the purchase of bonds, but they appreciated their father's thrift in later years when the bonds were divided among them.

There were plenty of chores in a farmhouse that had five fireplaces, but there was time for Charles to learn to play the violin as well as to complete his education at the Walpole Public High School. When the family moved from Walpole to Newton Upper Falls, he enrolled for a course in pattern-making at the Petee Iron Works,[3] as his elder brothers had done, though they had studied different branches of mechanics. When he had completed his courses, Charles joined John and George in their shop which manufactured iron products. A letter written on July 28, 1848, survives from that period.

> Dear Father
>
> As the next quarterly term of the savings institution commences next month I have thought it advisable to make a little effort to effect a deposit and agreeable to that intention I send by George the amount of twenty dollars which I wish you would deposit for me if you think it advisable.

---

[3] When some of the journeymen courses given at the Petee Iron Works began to be offered at the Massachusetts Institute of Technology, the firm discontinued the courses.

Business is so driving that I hardly find time to stop and sleep and much less to go avisiting in, so that I cannot make much calculation about going home to get some berries and milk but perhaps if you could make it convenient to call this way some Saturday I would try to make you a short visit.

George will tell the news etc. better than I can write it. Give my best respects to mother and Margaret and tell them to look out for the berries and milk when they see me coming. I do not know if you can make out to read this for it has been written in great haste, perhaps my ragged breeches will explain the reason why.

From your son
Charles Gould

A year earlier, on June 22, 1847, Charles had been married to Betsey Starbird of Maine, and the union had been blessed with a daughter, Ida. On Thanksgiving Day, November 30, 1848, Major Gould noted in his journal that "Charles, with his wife and child, were at home and passed the day with us." The fact that nothing is said about the California venture is negative evidence that it had not yet been conceived.

Charles Gould's early life was considerably happier and more secure than that of David Jackson Staples. David was born in Medway, Massachusetts, in 1824, and spent his infancy in Maryland.[4] His father, a machinist, was employed at a cotton mill near Baltimore. When David was ten his mother died of tuberculosis, and his two younger sisters and brother went to live with their Aunt Deborah in Massachusetts. David and his father moved to Lancaster, Pennsylvania, where both worked in a mill that manufactured cotton goods. A year later David's father died, also a victim of tuberculosis. He had been a Mason, and the Masonic order extended help to the orphaned boy.

---

[4] Information about David Staples' early life from his own account in the Staples Papers, C-D 288, the Bancroft Library, University of California, Berkeley. All quotations are from this source.

In later years David Staples recalled the kindnesses bestowed on him by the people of Lancaster, but he recalled even more vividly what had happened the day his father was buried. "It seems to me," he wrote, "that we had no sooner gotten in the house when we returned from the cemetery than all the relatives began dividing up the children." No one wanted the eleven-year-old David. One of his aunts suggested that he be apprenticed to learn a trade, and that whatever he earned should be turned over for the care of his sisters and his brother Fred.

David went out into the yard to think things over. He remembered his mother's advice that he should become a farmer, as this would keep him outdoors, and accordingly he decided to look for a home on a farm.

> I went inside [he wrote], wrapped up my clothes in a bundle, hoisted it over my shoulder and started on my way. Walking toward Rehobeth, I looked wistfully at each farm I passed. I did not seem able to walk up to the door and explain my plan. It was getting late and I was tired and hungry when a nice-looking farm came into view. The farmer was at the gate, watching his cows nip the grass that grew along the fence. I approached him with fear and trembling, and said "Good evening, sir." He answered "Good evening, my lad."

Encouraged by the farmer's manner, David told his story and was invited to have supper and spend the night, although the farmer said that he did not need any help. David put down his bundle and set to work on the evening chores with a will, and again the next morning he helped with the chores. The upshot was that the farmer told him that he had reconsidered and would like to have David remain with them. He could stay until he was fourteen, have a new suit of clothes each year, and attend school for three months during the winter. (Up to this time, he had had less than six months of schooling.) The unwritten contract included the provision that David called the farmer and his wife

13

"Pa" and "Ma." As it turned out, "Ma" was less congenial than "Pa."

While on the farm, David became acquainted with John Leach, a shoemaker in North Bridgeport, who "spun orations on philosophy" while he worked. David visited him at every opportunity and when he was fourteen apprenticed himself to Leach, not because he wanted to be a shoemaker but because he would have lots of time to listen to Leach. "To him I owe whatever may be in me of a higher nature," Staples declared later. "This man inspired me with hope and pointed out the way which was within reach."

The apprenticeship was completed in three years, but for some time David had realized that the confining work was beginning to tell on his health. He consulted a doctor who advised him to buy a tent and camping equipment and spend the summer in the open. With money he had earned working after he had completed his daily stint and on Saturday, which was a "free day," he acquired camping gear and a gun and spent the summer on Nantucket Island. At this time he became an excellent marksman.

When the summer was over, David was much improved in health and signed up for an apprentice course at the Petee Iron Works, also attending night school. When he came to put down his recollections, he wrote of the opportunity such schooling offered to "men like myself who have been handicapped by lack of education." Subsequently he completed a course in the construction of railroad engines at the Taunton Iron Works and received his engineering papers. On April 20, 1848, he married Mary Pratt Winslow, a sister of George Winslow, the third of the four founders of the Boston-Newton company.

George Winslow was born on August 11, 1823, at Ramapo, New York, the son of Eleazar Winslow, a descendent of Kenelm Winslow, a younger brother of Edward Winslow, who came to America on the *Mayflower* and who was a governor of the Plymouth Colony. Eventually the family moved to Newton Upper Falls, Massachusetts, and George, seeking to learn his father's trade

14

of machinist and molder, enrolled at the Petee Iron Works. In 1843 his sister Clarissa married Brackett Lord, the fourth of the group which first met at the iron works on that historic morning in 1841 and which eight years later resolved to seek their fortunes in California.

It is not known which of the four men was the first to suggest the formation of a California company—at the rate the gold fever was spreading it is quite possible they came down with it simultaneously—and little documentary evidence has survived about the actual organization of the company. The idea of a joint stock association was that a group would pool its assets, such as money, equipment, and labor, to achieve a common objective. Although the constitution of the Boston-Newton company has never come to light, it undoubtedly was similar to those of the scores of other companies being formed that winter. In fact, it has been conjectured that a prominent Boston attorney devised a standard form, which was sold to company organizers. In the case of the Boston-Newton Joint Stock Association, members were assessed three hundred dollars each, payable in two installments.[5] This sum would cover passage to Independence, Missouri, by rail and steamer and would pay for equipment for the overland journey and for supplies which would be sent to San Francisco by boat.

Most organized groups hailing from Boston banned liquor, gambling, and swearing, and also travel on Sunday. They were to stop and observe the Sabbath on the trail unless to do so might endanger the lives of the men or the animals. For infraction of these rules or other evidence of bad conduct, a member could be expelled and his share forfeited if two-thirds of a company's members so voted.

After the decision to form the company, the obvious first step was to recruit a complement of men. In the case of the Boston-Newton company, we can be sure that recruiting began with

---

[5] The receipt for one of the payments, signed by Jesse Winslow, is inserted between the leaves of Charles Gould's diary.

members of the founders' own families. George Gould, the second of the three Gould brothers, was one of the first to join up;[6] and Fred Staples, the younger brother of David, was another early recruit. In the Winslow family, there was Jesse, an uncle of George Winslow, and Benjamin Burt, Jr., a nephew of Jesse and cousin of George. Robert Coffey, who was best man at the wedding of Mary Winslow to David Staples, also signed on. This group may be regarded as the nucleus of the company which eventually numbered twenty-five, thirteen from the Newton area[7] and twelve from Boston.

All four founders lived in Newton Upper Falls, and probably the first meetings were held in their homes. Later, as the group grew in size, they may well have met at the home of Jesse Winslow, who had a large house in Newton Center. Later still, some of the meetings were held in Boston, where the company apparently rented a room to store the goods and equipment to be shipped west as well as the gear they would carry with them. Recruiting of members was probably informal; no doubt first they approached neighbors in Newton, some of whom may have enlisted acquaintances in Boston. I could find no evidence that the company ever advertised for members, and surely they would have had no difficulty in finding interested persons. Reuben Cole Shaw, a member of the Mount Washington Mining Company, which left for the gold fields on April 17, 1849, the day after the departure of the Boston-Newton company, has written that when the California fever struck the staid old New England metropolis

> the only remedy seemed to be a change of climate with the least possible delay. As the reports of the wonderful dis-

[6] In mid-March, George Gould changed his mind and did not travel west with the company.

[7] In Massachusetts, a town is comparable to a township in many other states. Newton was a town comprising fourteen villages, six of which include Newton as part of the name—Newton Upper Falls, Newton Lower Falls, Newton Center, Newton Highland, Newtonville, and West Newton.

covery of gold were fully confirmed, everybody became excited. Merchants closed out their business, clerks left their employers, mechanics packed their tools, lawyers gave up their practice, preachers bade adieu to their flocks and all joined the grand procession. Over twenty thousand persons left Boston for California in '49. . . .[8]

Another forty-niner, writing of those who succumbed to the gold fever, observed in his trail diary: "The people are of all kinds, some of the first people in the United States are a-going and some of the meanest are also along."[9] Yet although, as David Staples noted in his first journal entry, the members of the Boston-Newton company were "strangers with few acceptions," the organizers seem to have succeeded to an unusual degree in recruiting men who, whatever their other differences, were alike in being decent citizens, sober, upright, and God-fearing. They were just such a group as that described in the following notice, which appeared in the Boston *Traveller* on January 31, 1849.

HO! FOR CALIFORNIA

The undersigned being desirous to embark for California would like to be one of twelve or twenty-five Young Men who are possessed of good moral principles and who in the spirit of mutual benefit would have the good of each other in view, and would be willing to pledge themselves to exercise brotherly care over each other in adversity as well as in prosperity. Any such willing to leave for the Land of Promise, and willing to unite in the enterprise, may hear of one who stands ready to abide by his principles, by addressing Franklin, at this office.

[8] Reuben Cole Shaw, *Across the Plains in Forty-nine*, edited by Milo Milton Quaife (Chicago: The Lakeside Press, 1948), p. 10.

[9] "Diary of the Overland Trail, 1849, and Letters 1849–50 of Captain David DeWold," *Transactions of the Illinois Historical Society*, No. 32 (1925), p. 186.

It would be pleasant to record that "the undersigned" became one of the Boston-Newton party, but there is no Franklin on the company roster.

Good health as well as good character would be another factor that was considered in recruitment. Reuben Shaw wrote that applicants for membership in the Mount Washington company were "subjected to rigid examination by the surgeon and many rejected on account of physical disability";[10] but there is no evidence that such an examination was a prerequisite to membership in the Boston-Newton company. Just plain common sense would dictate their excluding anyone who did not appear to be physically capable of sustaining the rigors of a long and arduous journey. All but one of the men in the party were in the prime of life, the single exception being Jesse Winslow, who was fifty-five, although he gave his age as forty-eight.

A third factor was the possession of skills that would be useful on the trail. Each group sought to recruit men who could repair splintered wagon tongues, axles, and wheels, and mechanics, carpenters, blacksmiths, and wheelwrights were in great demand. During the organizational phase, a few men were needed who could handle business transactions competently, but on the trail the great need was for men with mechanical and manual skills. Professional men who wanted to travel overland had to be able to make themselves useful in ways alien to their callings, except for medical men. It was the custom to give physicians their transportation to California, and almost every company had one and sometimes two doctors. Dean Jewett Locke, a senior at Harvard Medical School, became the physician of the Boston-Newton company, and in fact the company delayed its departure so that Locke could complete his courses there.

---

[10] Shaw, *Across the Plains in Forty-nine*, p. 12. Shaw added that "it is a noteworthy fact that those who seemed the most robust and, to all appearances, best able to battle with the hardships of the journey, were the first to succumb to disease and death."

At a meeting held when all, or nearly all, of the company had been recruited, an election of officers was held. Brackett Lord, the eldest of the four founders, was elected president, and Walton Cheever Welch, who ran a print shop in Boston, was elected vice president. The secretary of the company was S. D. Osborn, on whom no information is available, and the treasurer was Jesse Winslow. The directors were Harvey Dickinson, Benjamin C. Evans, James A. Hough, and Thomas H. McGrath, all of Boston, and David Staples and Albion Sweetzer from the Newton area.[11]

The first major decision confronting a California company was the route it would travel. Seafaring, as native a mode of travel to New Englanders as air is to birds, dictated the choice for many forty-niners, and of 151 ships sailing from Boston in 1849, 102 carried companies of gold seekers. The first vessel to depart from Boston with an organized company was the *Edward Everett*, carrying the Boston and California Joint Stock and Trading Company.[12] The ship was named for the president of Harvard, and he presented a hundred volumes to the ship's library along with an admonition to the company to "take your Bible in one hand and your New England civilization in the other and make your mark on that country." Reuben Shaw, in his account, noted that "the *Edward Everett*, a fine ship, left Boston about ten days before the date of our departure, with a company of three hundred men, besides her crew of twenty officers and sailors." The vessel encountered "terrible gales, extreme cold, dense fogs, snow and ice" while rounding Cape Horn, and "finally arrived at San Francisco after a voyage lasting five and a half months, with a very debilitated lot of passengers. I have many times congratulated myself because of the fact that I was not one of the passengers of the good ship *Edward Everett*."[13]

[11] A complete roster of the company, listing the men in alphabetical order and giving biographical information, will be found in Chapter 3.

[12] Allan Forbes and Ralph W. Eastman, *Other Yankee Ship Sailing Cards* (Boston: State Street Trust Co., 1949), p. 88.

[13] Shaw, *Across the Plains in Forty-nine*, pp. 14–15.

The shortest land-and-water route, that via Panama, was chosen by eleven companies sailing from Massachusetts.[14] This journey was in three stages: by sea to Panama, by land across the isthmus, and by sea again to San Francisco. Two steamers of the Pacific Mail Steamship Company, the *California* and the *Oregon*, provided service from Panama to California. Another land-and-water route, taken by eight companies, was via Mexico. The New England Pioneers, for example, went to New Orleans, took a schooner for Veracruz, whence they traveled to Mexico City and proceeded overland on horseback to San Francisco by way of Mazatlán.

Overland, there were two main routes west of the Missouri— the old Santa Fe Trail and the Oregon-California Trail. Beyond Santa Fe, the southern route passed over the Sierra de Los Membros to the headwaters of the Gila River, followed the river to its junction with the Colorado, and then crossed the desert and went northward to San Francisco. Very few companies from Massachusetts tried the Gila route. The favorite route was via the South Pass of the Rocky Mountains, and one authority has said that "probably nearly as many men entered California in '49 by this route as by all others combined."[15] This was the way chosen by the Boston-Newton company and by five of the companies leaving Boston during 1849. The others were: the Congress and California Mutual Protection Association, made up of fifty young men, mostly from Roxbury, organized as a military body; the Sagamore and Sacramento of Lynn, with fifty-two members, also organized as a military company; the Granite State and California Mining and Trading Company, organized in New Hampshire, numbering thirty men;[16] the Mount Wash-

[14] Information about routes and the companies that traveled them from Octavius Thorndike Howe, *Argonauts of '49* (Cambridge: Harvard University Press, 1923), pp. 12–45.

[15] *Ibid.*, p. 39.

[16] The Granite State company, like the Mount Washington company, left Boston on April 17, 1849, the day after the Boston-Newton company's

ington Mining Company, previously mentioned, with forty-one members; and the Ophir Company, a party of only fifteen.

Although the route followed by the Boston-Newton company is described phase by phase by Gould and Staples in their daily records, they do not provide an over-all, start-to-finish view, and it may be helpful to have a summary description of the Oregon-California Trail as it was given by Milo M. Quaife in his introduction to Reuben Shaw's account:

> Its easterly terminus was on some point or near the Missouri River such as Independence, St. Joseph, Fort Leavenworth, or Council Bluffs. To these starting points settlers from widely separated points in the Middle West or along the Atlantic Seaboard found their way, and presently all converged upon the Lower Platte River, up which and the North Platte they pursued their journey to the vicinity of Casper, Wyoming. Here they crossed to the eastward flowing Sweetwater, up which they continued to the famous South Pass of the Rockies in western Wyoming.
>
> After crossing this well-nigh imperceptible backbone of the continent the main road turned southwardly to Fort Bridger, which afforded the first civilized stopping-point west of Fort Laramie. From Fort Bridger the road turned northwardly again to Fort Hall, near present-day Pocatello, Idaho.
>
> At Fort Hall the Oregon Trail and the California Road separated. The former led on westwardly to and down the Columbia (Fort Hall was itself on the Snake or Lewis Fork of the Columbia) ; the California Road veered sharply southward to seek the headwaters of the St. Mary's or Humboldt River in northeastern Nevada, and descend this stream to

---

departure, and both are mentioned in the Gould and Staple journals. Kimball Webster of the Granite State group kept a journal which was published many years later under the title *The Gold Seekers of '49: A Personal Narrative of the Overland Trail and Adventures in California and Oregon from 1849 to 1854* (Manchester, N.H.: Standard Book Co., 1917).

the point where a crossing to the Carson was effected. Thence either by Carson River and Pass or by the Truckee River and Truckee or Donner Pass the Sierras were crossed, to debouch upon the mining area adjacent to the American and the Sacramento rivers.

There were, of course, important variations in the route we have thus outlined, two or three of which require present explanation. At South Pass, instead of following the main road via Fort Bridger to Fort Hall the emigrant might take the Greenwood, or Sublette, Cut-Off, which plunged directly westward across rivers and intervening desert to rejoin the main road on the upper Bear in southeastern Idaho. By the Cut-Off, a saving of several days' travel was effected, at the cost, however, of crossing a considerable stretch of desert, whereas the road by Fort Bridger was well-watered.

Another and earlier variation of the route from South Pass led northwardly into the Wind River Mountains, and by a devious trail impassable to wagons struck westwardly toward Fort Hall at some distance to the north of the Sublette Cut-Off as already described. . . .

All three of the routes from South Pass reunited on the upper Bear to run as one as far as Soda Springs. Near here, however, still many miles short of Fort Hall, in the summer of 1849 was opened Hudspeth's or the Emigrants' Cut-Off, which ran southwestwardly 120 miles to a point on upper Raft River where it intersected the California Road coming from Fort Hall. Although the distance saved by the Hudspeth Cut-Off was comparatively slight, as soon as it was opened practically all emigrants bound for California forsook the older route in favor of the new Cut-Off.

Numerous variations in the route from Raft River to the Humboldt were followed. Once arrived on the Humboldt itself, still other choices were open to the emigrant. Probably the great majority continued down the river past Carson Sink and across to Carson River, to cross the Sierras by either the Truckee (Donner) or the Carson Pass. But many left the Humboldt at the Great Bend (vicinity of Winnemucca) to proceed thence westward across the desert and the intervening Sierras to northern California, whence they made their way southward to the upper Sacramento.[17]

We do not know what impelled the Boston-Newton party to chose an overland route, but New Englanders' interest in transcontinental travel antedated the gold rush by a quarter of a century. A young Boston schoolteacher, Hall J. Kelley, was writing letters and newspaper articles in the early 1820's to urge that the United States assert her claim to the Oregon country, and the Oregon Emigration Society was organized in Lynn, Massachusetts, in 1838. Frémont's *Report of the Exploring Expedition to the Rocky Mountains in the Year 1842* was published in 1845; and Bryant's *What I Saw in California*, describing his journey across the continent in 1846–1847, also was available by the time the gold fever began to spread. Both were books to stir any young man's imagination. In addition, by 1849 several guidebooks were on the market. One of the most popular was J. Ely Sherwood's *Pocket Guide to California, Sea and Land Routes* (1849) containing valuable information and advice, some of which had been supplied by Bryant. It also included a map of the territories along the route to California via South Pass, but it was not easy to decipher because of the numerous feathery lines and the fine print. There also was Lansford W. Hastings' *Emigrants' Guide to Oregon and California* (1845), which was popular but dangerously misleading in some of its details; and William Clayton's *The Latter Day Saints Emigrant Guide from Council Bluffs to the Valley of the Great Salt Lake* (1848), which included accurate distances between points and authentic descriptions. On some of the maps then available the mileage was given, but on the trail it was difficult to estimate the distance between points.

---

[17] Shaw, *Across the Plains in Forty-nine*, pp. xx–xxiii.

In 1849 there were three instruments that registered mileage—the odometer, the roadmeter, and the viameter. They calculated the turns of the wagon wheel and by multiplying this number by the circumference of the wheel, mileage could be computed. The Boston-Newton party probably did not carry such an instrument, since Gould, referring to the distance traveled, frequently says "we think" or "we suppose."

Once a company had decided whether it would travel by land or sea, the members were ready to begin the crucially important task of purchasing supplies and equipment. With visions of the riches awaiting them at the end of their journey, many of the argonauts' first thought no doubt was of mining equipment and they would begin their purchases with such items as those described in the following advertisements.[18]

☞ FOR CALIFORNIA.—Superior Gold Washing Sieves and Wire cloth—Wrought Iron Fry Pans, Tin Plates—Drinking Cups—Canteens—Fine scales for weighing gold—assortment of goods suitable for that market —for sale by Whiting & Brother, No. 31 Union Street.

[18] The first two advertisements appeared in the Boston *Post* on March 19, 1849, the third in the Boston *Traveller* on February 3, 1849.

»»»» CALIFORNIA GOLD «««««

The sifter and washer combined, both operations being performed by one motion, invented and manufactured and for sale by WATERMAN, at his Kitchen Furnishing Wareroom, 83 and 85 Cornhill, where all on the eve of departure for the gold regions, will find their personal outfit of tin ware, &c. &c.

»»»» FOR CALIFORNIA «««««

For sale, a large assortment of Shovels, Spades, Hoes, Ploughs, Pick Axes, Miner's Picks, Crow Bars, Canal Barrows, Stoves, &c., particularly adapted to the California markets, and which we offer in large or small quantities, as desired, and at extremely low prices.

Also—all kinds of Garden, Field and Grass Seeds.

David Prouty & Co.
19 & 20 North Market street

Unfortunately, many forty-niners overlooked the fact that before they could prospect for gold they would have to reach their destination, and many cumbersome mining devices were discarded along the trail as it became necessary to lighten the wagons. When the Mount Washington company reached the foothills of the Rockies, according to Reuben Shaw, a large auger, with a very elaborate extension stem, with which we had intended to prospect the lower regions to any desired depth for the yellow metal, was left in the foothills, and a lot of sheet-iron gold-washers, made for the purpose of separating large quantities of gold from the shining sands, found a resting place in the Platte River. Either of the above would have been about as useful as a Texas steer in a China shop.[19]

Similarly, when the Granite State company was trying to lighten its load as early on the trail as Fort Kearny, in present Nebraska, some of the men argued that it was impractical to pack heavy spades and picks and a filter weighing thirty pounds "2000 miles on the sore backs of mules." The majority of the party opposed discarding the filter, but eventually the man on whose mule it was packed got rid of the thing by hiding it in a thicket.[20]

Another common mistake of the argonauts was to overburden themselves with provisions; and here again the newspapers of the day give us an idea of the kinds of supplies that were offered for sale to the forty-niners.[21]

```
»»»»» ST. LOUIS FLOUR «««««
Landing from bark Brazil, at Battery wharf.
        750 bbls. McElroy & Co. Brand
        250    "   Tibbet & Co.'s.     "
For sale by              Howard, Son & Co.
                         27 Central wharf.
```

[19] Shaw, *Across the Plains in Forty-nine*, pp. 55–56.

[20] Webster, *The Gold Seekers of '49*, pp. 49 and 61.

[21] The first and last advertisements appeared in the Boston *Traveller* on January 31, 1849, the remainder in the Boston *Post* on March 19, 1849.

☞ BREAD FOR CALIFORNIA.—A constant supply of Pilot and Navy Bread, kiln dried for shipment, for sale by THOS. WATTSON & SONS, at their Bakery, Fort Hill Wharf.

»»»»» CALIFORNIA STORES ««««« 10,000 POUNDS sugar cured Hams; 10,000 new Pea Beans; also Beef, Pork, Lard, Butter, Cheese &c., for sale by BALDWIN & STONE, 9 Market square.

»»»»» MALAGA RAISINS ««««« 1200 BOXES Lunch Muscatel Raisins—200 casks blue mark Sun do—for sale by SILAS PIERCE & CO. 22 Elm st.

»»»»» ZANTA CURRANTS ««««« 160 bbls. fresh landing—for sale by SILAS PIERCE & CO. 22 Elm st.

»»»»» PORK, LARD, HAMS «««««
32 TIERCES LARD
18 bbls Mess PORK
8 tierces HAMS
5 do SHOULDERS
20 bbls. CASTOR OIL
landing from ship James Perkins, and for sale by

Howard, Son & Co.
27 Central wharf.

Also, of course, there was the matter of clothing and weapons. The "military bodies" wore uniforms, which they had a chance to display when they paraded, as was customary for California companies before leaving Boston. The Congress and California Mutual Protection Association, which was described as "one of the largest and best appointed companies," and which "took with them four musicians, two colored servants, and six dogs," had uniforms of light gray banded with gold.[22] Prepared for most any eventuality, they were armed with rifles, revolvers, bowie knives, and sabers. Another company, the Sagamore and Sacramento of Lynn, was said to have made "a fine show as they marched down State Street in their gray uniforms trimmed with silver braid, and a band of music ahead. Each man was armed with rifle, revolver, and sheath knife. Their wagons, of which they had one to every four men, all made to order, were drawn by four horses resplendent in silver-plated harnesses and from the rear of each wagon projected a swivel gun."

---

[22] The description of the two companies is quoted from Howe, *Argonauts of '49*, pp. 41–42. Despite its sumptuous accouterments, the Congress and California company did not fare very well; it broke up after reaching Westfield, Missouri.

28

For those who did not wear uniforms, one of the most popular outfits consisted of a knee-length topcoat, pants tucked inside high boots, and a broad-brimmed felt hat. A daguerreotype of Charles Gould taken in the suit of clothes he bought for the California trip shows a topcoat with a wide collar that could have been velvet. Around his neck he is wearing a large red silk handkerchief, an item of apparel which also was popular for the "California Rig." Indeed, a young man with a long purse could virtually fill a prairie schooner with his California wardrobe, arms, camping equipment, and personal articles, as the following contemporaneous advertisements suggest.[23]

»»» OUTFITS FOR CALIFORNIA «««
At Bowen & Brother's, for TEN DOLLARS, including Shirts, Socks, Money Belt, Under Garments, Cravats, Braces, Buck Mittens or Gloves.

Bowen & Brother.
97 Washington street.

»»» CALIFORNIA HATS AND CAPS «««
Straw, Leghorn, Panama, and Palm Leaf Hats, at 11 and 13 Washington street, foot of Cornhill, Boston.

M. P. Elliott.

[23] The first three advertisements appeared in the Boston *Traveller*, January 31, 1849; the fourth and fifth in the Boston *Post*, March 19, 1849; and the sixth and seventh in the *Traveller*, February 3, 1849.

»»»» FOR CALIFORNIA ««««
Both Colt's and Allen's Revolvers, and a large
assortment of other Sporting Articles, for
sale by
James Eaton
No. 44 Washington street

☞ GUNPOWDER FOR CALIFORNIA.
Superior quality Gunpowder, made by the
American Powder Company, in kegs and
canisters of various sizes, suitable for blast-
ing, sporting, cannons &c. Orders promptly
executed by WM. C. FAY, No. 49 India
Wharf, south side.

»»»» TO KEEP DRY FEET ««««
INNER SOLES of thin GUTTA PERCHA is
a most excellent article to place inside the
Shoe or Boot, it being a non conductor of
electricity, and retains the natural warmth of
the foot. For sale at the Rubber Wareroom,
No. 94 Washington street.
P.S. Extra sizes cut out to order.
J. Haskins

»»» CALIFORNIA RUBBER GOODS ««« of every description made expressly for those going to that country, of the patent Metallic Vulcanized Rubber. The subscriber is constantly receiving from the Roxbury Factory and other establishments, at the Wareroom, 94 Washington Street, useful articles for that open country, unaffected by any climate. These Goods are just what is wanted by the exploring parties, emigrating to the Gold regions.

Among the goods are the following, viz:— Coats and Capes—Caps and Southwesters— Pants and Leggings—Wading Boots—do Pants—Camp Blankets—Provision Bags—Air Beds—Air Pillows and Cushions—Water Bottles—Canteens—Life Preservers—Clothing Bags—Knapsacks—Haversacks—Saddle Bags—Gun and Pistol Cases—Gloves and Mitts—Wagon Covers—Drinking Cups—&c. &c. Outfits to all parts of the world of these Goods, and warranted not to decompose. Trading and Mining Companies will find it to their advantage to purchase at the Rubber Wareroom, 94 Washington street.

J. Haskins

»»»» FOR CALIFORNIA «««««

A fine assortment of Indispensable Articles
of Stationery, such as Portable Desks—Dress-
ing Cases—Manifold Letter Writer—Metallic
Mem. Books—Diaries—Blank Journal Books
—Account Books—Paper of all kinds—Gold,
Steel and Quill Pens—Ink—Knives—Razors
—Razor Straps—Shaving Soap and Brushes—
with many other articles of utility. For sale
in large or small lots, very cheap for cash, at
MARSH'S
77 Washington street
Joy's Building

Perhaps this last advertisement came to the attention of Charles
Gould's family, for on the eve of his departure to California
Major Gould gave him a brown leather-bound diary and brothers
John and George gave him a portable writing desk.

The members of the association originally planned to work
together for two or three years, and they purchased two years'
supply of mining equipment and other goods to be shipped to San
Francisco via Cape Horn on the bark *Helen Augusta*. This vessel
had been acquired by the Merchants and Mining Company, and
plans were made to build a steamboat on its deck during the
voyage, enabling the passengers to go up the Sacramento River
when they reached California. The *Helen Augusta* sailed from
Boston in mid-May and reached San Francisco in mid-September.[24]

[24] Sources do not agree on the sailing and arrival dates. C. W. Haskins, in
The Argonauts of California (New York, 1890), p. 465, gives the sailing date
from Boston harbor as May 12. But according to a statement from Robert W.
Parkinson, West Coast correspondent for *Steamboat Bill of Facts*, the journal

In 1849 the Commonwealth of Massachusetts was still issuing passports. They were not obligatory for the Boston-Newton party, but they provided official identification and ten of the men paid the two-dollar fee to obtain one. They were impressive-looking documents bearing the seal of Massachusetts, and read as follows:

> TO ALL TO WHOM THESE PRESENTS
> SHALL COME, GREETING:
> I, GEORGE M. BRIGGS, Governor of the
> Commonwealth of Massachusetts, one of the
> United States of America, do hereby Request
> all whom it may concern, to permit safely and
> freely to pass [Name] of [Town], a citizen of the
> said Commonwealth, going to CALIFORNIA
> and elsewhere, and in case of need, to give him
> all lawful aid and protection.

A description giving the age, stature, complexion, and color of eyes and hair of the bearer was appended, and also his signature. Thus, from Charles Gould's passport we know that he stood five feet ten inches, had a light complexion, hazel eyes, and brown hair. The descriptions of the others who held passports are given in the company roster in Chapter 3.

The company had originally planned to leave on April 1, but they postponed their departure for two weeks in order to enable

---

of the Steamship Historical Society of America, August 27, 1949, "The *Helen Augusta* sailed from Boston May 14, and arrived in San Francisco October 31, 1849. A manuscript in the California Historical Society by G. W. Young, describes the voyage on this vessel and tells of the prefabrication of the steamboat and its machinery on the deck of the bark while en route. Mr. Young was a member of the Massachusetts Mining Company." However, the October 31 date is almost certainly an error, for the arrival of the bark *Ellen* [sic] *Augusta* on September 14 is listed in the San Francisco *Pacific News* on September 18, 1849, and on October 27, 1849, the clearance of the vessel for Valparaiso is noted. A list of the goods shipped on the *Helen Augusta* has not been found.

Dean Locke to finish up his medical studies. In the end this worked to their advantage, since the grass on the prairies was not high enough to provide forage until the second week in May. However, it was unwise to delay departure too long, for if a party did not reach the mountains before snow started it would be in trouble. One of the directors, Harvey Dickinson, was to remain in Boston for an additional week to take care of business matters for the company. Traveling alone with light luggage, he would have no difficulty securing accommodations on any train or boat, and he would rejoin the group at St. Joseph, Missouri, before they started across the plains.

As the date of departure for California drew near, relatives of the gold seekers held family gatherings to bid them godspeed. On April 8, Major Gould noted in his journal.

> My children were all at home, and in good health. The cause of this was that Charles, my youngest son, has joined a company of men by the name of the Boston & Newton Joint Stock Association, who intend to leave these parts immediately and proceed to Upper California to engage in the gold business. This was an interesting occasion to me. Charles will, in all probability, be absent two or three years, and taking into consideration the changes which usually take place in a family at such a period, it must be very doubtful about my ever having the satisfaction of seeing all my children together again.

It was on this occasion that Charles was presented with the diary and the portable writing desk.

On Friday, April 13, all members of the company assembled in Boston, and on Saturday came the parade down State Street, with each member dressed in full California rig, flags flying and a band playing. On Sunday the company marched in a body to church to hear words of admonition and advice and prayers for a safe journey and good fortune at the end of it. On Monday,

April 16, they arrived early at the railroad station to start on the first leg of their journey.

In 1849, the Boston and Albany railway was celebrating its eighth birthday, and it was still quite a novelty to travel aboard the red cars which clicked over the tracks at the unheard-of speed of eighteen miles an hour. The train would carry them to Greenbush, New York, on the east bank of the Hudson, and since no railroad bridge as yet spanned the river at this point, they would be ferried across the river to Albany.

The company's gear made a small mountain on the station platform. It included tents, air mattresses, rubber blankets as well as woolen ones, rain clothes, a stove, a collapsible rubber boat, saddles, harnesses, various tools, canned goods, and a supply of medicine. Each man was allowed a small trunk and a carpet-bag carrying articles for use on the journey to St. Joseph. After they had supervised the loading of the luggage, there were last minute farewells and handshakes and tearful embraces from the womenfolk; then at the conductor's "All Aboard!" the men climbed into their private car which carried a placard: THE BOSTON-NEWTON JOINT STOCK ASSOCIATION. The engine bell clanged, and to the accompaniment of shouted good-byes and cheers the train pulled slowly out.[25]

25 On April 17, 1849, under the heading "More Overland Companies," the *Daily Overland Traveller* noted: "The Boston-Newton Joint Stock Association started yesterday for California overland, by way of St. Louis and Fort Independence." The item also included the names of the officers and director.

CHAPTER 3

The Boston-Newton Company Roster

Here, in alphabetical order, is the roster of the Boston-Newton Joint Stock Association as it was constituted when it left Boston. Summary biographical information is included.[1] Variant spellings of many of the names (*Ayers* for *Ayer*; *Dickenson* for *Dickinson*, etc.) appear in the diaries, letters, and other primary materials used in this book. These variant forms have been allowed to stand in all quoted material, but the spellings given below are the correct ones.

MILO J. AYER
Born in Vermont, Ayer was twenty-nine when he left for California. Not only was he a strict temperance man, but he refrained from smoking, gambling, and swearing. Probably his most memorable characteristic was his correct manner of speech. Ayer was skilled in two trades—he was a carpenter and a millwright. His wife, Phoebe, was a member of the Bradford family of *Mayflower* fame. At this time they had two children—a son and a daughter.

---

[1] For the sources of the biographical information in this chapter, see A Note on Sources.

BENJAMIN BURT, JR.

Born in Freetown, Massachusetts, Burt was a graduate of Bridgewater Normal School and a schoolmaster before he signed up for the trip to California. The son of a deacon, he was a cousin of George Winslow and a nephew of Jesse Winslow. He was unmarried.

ROBERT COFFEY

A Bostonian by birth, Robert Coffey moved to Newton. He worked as a mechanic before joining the Boston-Newton company venture. In 1848 he had been best man at the wedding of David Staples and Mary Winslow.

HARVEY DICKINSON

A director of the company. Dickinson was born in Massachusetts, and was twenty-seven in 1849. He had once ventured as far west as Ohio.

DANIEL E. EASTERBROOK

Born in Exeter, England in 1829, Easterbrook was an infant when his parents joined a group emigrating to the United States. The family settled first in Connecticut, then moved to Needham, Massachusetts. He studied under Mary Fuller, well known for her work as a horticulturist, and became exceptionally skilled in tree surgery. He was working in this field when news of the gold strike reached Boston. Easterbrook was the youngest member of the party—he was not yet twenty when the company left for California.

BENJAMIN C. EVANS

A director of the company. Evans was a native of Roxbury, Massachusetts. The passport he carried to California gave his age as thirty in 1849. He is described as being five feet six and a quarter inches; complexion dark; eyes hazel; hair auburn.

WALTON CHEEVER FELCH

Vice president of the company. Felch was born in Massachusetts, the son of a prominent Boston physician, and was thirty-two in

1849. By nature he was artistic and meticulous, and his innate good will drew people to him. He had studied art and ran a print shop in Boston. Although the shop was prospering, he sold it when he joined the Boston-Newton company. According to his passport, he was five feet six and three-quarters inches in height; complexion light; eyes gray; hair light. Felch was married, but had no children.

CHARLES GOULD

A founder of the company. Charles Gould was born in Walpole, Massachusetts, on April 3, 1824. He attended the Walpole Public High School, and took a course in pattern-making at the Petee Iron Works. He was working with his two older brothers in their shop which manufactured metal products when he heard the news of the California gold strike. Charles was married to the former Betsey Starbird, and had a daughter, Ida. (For additional biographical details, see Chapter 2.)

JAMES A. HOUGH

A director of the company. According to his passport, Hough was thirty-one in 1849; height five three and one-half inches; complexion dark; eyes dark; hair dark.

DEAN JEWETT LOCKE

The physician of the company. Locke, who was twenty-six the day the group left Boston, was born at Langdon, Connecticut, the son of Luther Locke and Hannah Willard. (Mrs. Locke's brother Josiah was the father of the famous educator Frances Willard.) When he was fourteen he arranged to earn his tuition at an academy in a neighboring town by doing janitorial work; he earned his room and board by doing chores for a resident of the town. After his graduation he taught school for several terms, working as a farmhand in the summer to earn money for further study. He became a protégé of Horace Mann, and was a member of the first class to graduate from Bridgewater Normal School. He then taught a few terms until he had enough money to matriculate at Harvard Medical School. The Boston-Newton company postponed its departure as long as possible so that Locke could complete his senior work there. By nature he was gentle, pleasant, soft-spoken, and extremely fond of children and young people. According to his passport, he was five feet ten, had brown hair, blue-gray eyes, and a fair complexion. He was unmarried at this time.

BRACKETT LORD

A founder of the company and its president. Lord was born at Ossipee, New Hampshire, January 4, 1819, the son of Wentworth and Sally Lord. In 1841 he signed up for an apprenticeship course at the Petee Iron Works. In 1843, he married George Winslow's sister, Clarissa, and at the time the company left for California the Lords had a daughter and a son.

NATHANIEL B. LORING

Loring was born in 1810 at Pembroke, Massachusetts, the son of Nathaniel Loring and Catharine Smith Loring. In 1849 he was living in Newton, was married, and had a daughter, Emily, and a son, Edwin. According to his passport, he stood five feet eight and a half, had gray eyes, light hair, and a light complexion.

THOMAS H. MCGRATH (or MeGrath)

A director of the company. McGrath was from Massachusetts.

WILLIAM H. NICHOLS

A bachelor, Nichols was thirty-two when he left for the gold fields. He had been a resident of Newton, where he was a member of the Unitarian Church and a member of the Newton lodge of the Independent Order of Odd Fellows. According to his passport, Nichols' height was five feet seven inches; complexion light; eyes blue; hair auburn.

HARRY NOYES

No definite information is available on Harry Noyes.

S. D. OSBORN
Secretary of the company. No information available.

DAVID J. STAPLES
A founder of the company and a director. Staples, who was twenty-five in 1849, was born in Medway, Massachusetts, and spent his early years in Maryland. He had taken an apprenticeship course at the Petee Iron Works and a course in constructing locomotives at the Taunton Iron Works, and held a responsible position with a firm that made railroad engines. On April 20, 1848, he had married Mary Pratt Winslow, a sister of George Winslow; a daughter, Elizabeth, was born to them while he was enroute to the gold fields. His passport describes Staples as six feet and a quarter inch in height; complexion light; eyes hazel; hair sandy. (For additional biographical details, see Chapter 2.)

JOHN FREDERICK STAPLES
The younger brother of David Staples, who was about twenty-one in 1849, was known as Fred. He was a resident of Upper Newton Falls at this time.

ALBION C. SWEETZER
A director of the company. Sweetzer, who was thirty in 1849, was a contractor and had just lost $4,000 in a building speculation in Boston when he joined the company. According to his passport, his height was five feet eleven and a half inches; complexion light; eyes blue; hair auburn. He was unmarried at this time.

GEORGE THOMASON
The cook for the company. Thomason was born in England and had just received his citizenship papers when he joined the company. It is not known if he was an experienced cook. Thomason was married.

JOHN WHITE
From the Boston area.

41

LEWIS K. WHITTIER

From the Boston area. Whittier was twenty-seven in 1849.

JAMES ST. CLAIRE WILSON

Wilson was a resident of Roxbury and was twenty-seven in 1849. He was listed as a trader, was married, and had a son, James, and a daughter, Mary. According to his passport, he had brown hair, blue eyes, and a light complexion, and was a half-inch under six feet.

GEORGE WINSLOW

A founder of the company. Descended from a distinguished New England family, George Winslow was the son of Eleazar Winslow, and was born at Ramapo, New York, on August 11, 1823. Subsequently, the family moved to Newton Upper Falls, where George learned his father's trade—machinist and molder—and met his future co-founders of the Boston-Newton Company when he was apprenticed to the Petee Iron Works. In 1845 he was married and had one child, a son, at the time he left for California. A second son was born two months after his departure.

JESSE WINSLOW

Treasurer of the company. Although Winslow's age was given by David Staples as forty-eight, according to the Winslow Genealogy he was born on May 25, 1794, so was in fact fifty-five. Since men over fifty were considered too old for trail travel, no doubt Winslow felt it necessary to shade matters a bit. He was the oldest member of the party. In 1823 he moved to Newton Upper Falls, where he held several public offices—postmaster, assessor, and selectman; in addition, he served in the Massachusetts State Legislature (1839–1840). In 1830 Winslow married Caroline Ray; they had no children. At one time a Baptist, he later joined the Unitarian Church, sang in the choir, and played a trumpet in the church orchestra. William H. Nichols (see above) also played in this orchestra. Jesse Winslow was an uncle of George Winslow.

CHAPTER 4

Boston to Independence

I

The first lines that Charles Gould recorded in the brown diary
his father had given him were:

> Left Boston April 16, 1849, at 8 o'clock—weather clear
> and cold—arrived at Springfield at 1 without any circum-
> stances of importance. Was delayed until 10 minutes before
> 4 o'clock by a freight train having run off the track, but after
> a pleasant trip we reached Greenbush at ¼ past nine and
> were soon ensconced in Jenkinsons. Rail Road House in
> Albany where we enjoyed the comforts and luxuries of our
> fair landlady's good [hospitality?].

David Staples' comments were somewhat more circumstantial:

> Left the city of Boston a member of the Boston and
> Newton Joint Stock Association bound for *California* for the
> purpose of bettering our condition on money matters and
> seeing the country. I left home with regret as it is no easy
> matter for me to leave *wife, home, friends,* and attachments.
> The company numbered 26 members made up of people

43

from Boston and Newton.[1] We started from the Western
Depot at ¼ past 8 o'clock and had a car to ourselves through
to Albany. Being detained in Springfield we arrived at
Albany at 9 o'clock. Nothing of note occurred on the way.
We now begin to see the developments of the character of
the men. We are strangers with few acceptions, but a remarkable trait in Americans is to have confidence and respect
for each other and only on being disappointed or deceived do
they distrust their ability or zeal to opperate together. We
shall know more of each other after we have passed the
bounds of civilization and camped together on the Western
Prara.

Albany was the transportation center for the entire north-
eastern region, and its station and hotels were jammed with
travelers during the early spring of 1849. A special emigrant train
had been put into service to take care of the increased traffic
westward. After an overnight stay the Boston-Newton party began
the next leg of their journey at 12:30 on April 17, having secured
tickets through from Albany to Cincinnati.

The day [wrote Charles Gould] is remarkably fine and warm
and the contrast seemed quite pleasing from the cold weather
of yesterday. After much trouble and *dickering* we succeeded
in procuring a car for ourselves provided we allowed 10
other emmigrants to go with us and we were very fortunate
in having good company. Arrived at Schenectady at 2 and
stopped until 3½ o'clock. Kept going all night and next day,
April 18th, until 2 P.M., when we arrived at Buffalo and
after some delay we took passage in the *Steamer Baltic* for
Sandusky, Ohio, advertised to start at 7 P.M. Our journey
so far has been very pleasant and interesting, and although

---

[1] The company numbered 25 members (not 26, as Gould says), but only
24 left Boston on April 16; Harvey Dickinson remained behind to attend to
some business matters, catching up with the others on May 5.

we have had 2nd class fare, we have enjoyed ourselves very much.

It speaks well for the party's morale that Gould could refer to the trip as "pleasant"; at least by today's standards it would seem something of an ordeal. Trains made frequent stops to pick up fuel for the wood-burning steam engines—during which the passengers took the opportunity to disembark and get some exercise—and as night approached there was another stop while the trainmen lit the kerosene lamps on the front of the engine and inside the cars. (Until the introduction of these lamps in 1848 only a few freight trains moved after dark. To light their way, flares were burned on the sand-covered platform of a small car that was attached to the front of the engine and pushed along.) Even stopping the train was a fairly dramatic operation in 1849. After the brakeman applied the brakes at the front end of the first car, he rushed down the narrow aisle to set the brakes on the second car, and so on the length of the train. The cars were not heated, and no doubt the passengers welcomed the stop for breakfast at Rochester, which gave them a chance to get warm.

At Buffalo, emigrants arriving on the three daily trains from the East boarded steamers which would take them across Lake Erie to Sandusky, Ohio. When organized groups left the depot, attired in their California outfits, it was the custom to march four abreast down Buffalo's wide Exchange Street to the stone pier a few blocks away. The *Baltic*, on which the Boston-Newton party traveled, was a first-class steamer, well furnished and well equipped. She had been built in Buffalo two years before, and her maiden voyage had been musically celebrated with "The Baltic Waltz," dedicated to the captain, A. T. Kingman.

On the morning of April 19, en route to Sandusky, the *Baltic* put in at Erie, Pennsylvania. There Charles Gould wrote:

> . . . The water has been quite rough and some of our company have been troubled with sea sickness, but they have all put on a cheerful face this morning. There is a very large

company aboard the boat, every berth and sofa being occupied for the passengers to sleep upon. It has continued rough through the [day] and nearly every person has been sick. . . .

After their arrival in Sandusky, David Staples also wrote of their "having had a very rough time. This being the first trip of the Boat this season the officers and crew were nearly all sick as well as a large number of passengers. I was sick as need be and did not get over it under a day or two after landing."

Gould's diary entry for April 20 describes the arrival and carries the story of the journey forward:

We are now in full sight of Sandusky. The morning is beautiful, the waters are quite still, but we are fast upon a sand bar from which we did not get off until we had lain there about 6 hours, when we were taken off by a small steamer sent out for our relief, thus making 2 nights and 1½ days from Buffalo, the usual time being 20 hours. Our experience of travelling upon Lake Erie is not very agreeable and some of our company have suffered severely from sea sickness. We found Sandusky to be very pleasantly laid out upon elevated level land, very regularly laid out with wide streets, and bids fair to become a large and handsome city. We stopped here over night and started the next morning, April 21st, at 5 o'clock in the cars for Cincinnati and after travelling over a very level road, but laid with very poor rails,[2] through a very fertile and mostly a very beautiful country, we reached Cincinnati at 9 o'clock P.M. and put up at the Henrie House.[3]

[2] The railroad between Sandusky and Cincinnati was built on a narrow-gauge track, and the ride was neither so comfortable nor so speedy as that between Boston and Buffalo.

[3] Henrie House, proprietor L. Mount, was a first-class hotel of one hundred rooms located on Third Street between Main and Sycamore. See Charles Cist, *Cincinnati 1841* (Cincinnati: Wm. H. Moore & Co., 1841; reprinted 1851 and 1859). Because of the shortage of rooms, Osborn, Noyes, Loring, Thomason, and White lodged at another hotel.

Established in 1788, Cincinnati was one of the first settlements in the old Northwest Territory. It had been a military post, becoming a town after General "Mad Anthony" Wayne's victory at Fallen Timbers in 1794 and the 1795 treaty of Greenville ended Indian warfare in the Ohio Valley. Rivers were the arteries carrying the flow of westward settlement, and Cincinnati, situated on the north bank of the Ohio, was an important port of call from the days of keelboats and flatboats. In 1816 steam navigation was opened on the river, and with the completion, in 1830, of the Louisville and Portland Canal around the falls at Louisville, steamboat traffic traversed the entire thousand-mile length of the Ohio to the Mississippi. When gold fever swept the nation, several extra steamers were put in service to take care of the California-bound passengers. These boats did not run on a fixed schedule; they docked, let the passengers disembark, unloaded the freight, policed up, took on supplies and a new shipment of freight, and set out again. They were called "tramp steamers" and later, as traffic increased, were advertised as "Gold Rush Packets."

Both Gould and Staples were favorably impressed by what they had seen of the new country. Writing of the trip from Sandusky, Staples, in an entry dated April 21, observed rather wryly: "Houses mostly made of logs and to a New England man there is nothing very enticeing about them"; however, he thought "this must eventually be a populous country."

> [In Cincinnati] we stopped over Sunday. On Sunday we went to Church. Most of us attended meeting at the Christian Baptist and Orthodox. Heard good preaching at both places.
>
> Cincinnati is a great city on the Banks of the Ohio on nearly level land with the exception of that part next the river which is the same as the banks of all the western rivers— quite Bluff. There is some high ground back of the City on which some of us stroled. Here we had a chance to view Kentucky on one side, Ohio on the other; one free, the other

[a] slave state. Slave labor cannot compete with free labor in making things look thrifty.

Gould's account of that Sunday is dated April 22:

> We staid at the Henrie House this day and spent our time very pleasantly in examining the city, which we found to be very regularly laid out and having a very handsome appearance, but what appears very disgusting to eastern people is the filth, and the hogs which roam in the streets very plentifully and seem to have a perfect liberty throughout the city. Upon ascending upon a high hill called Mt. Adams, a perfect view of the entire city and the towns of Newport and Covington [Kentucky] on the opposite side of the river is obtained, which presents a view of rare beauty and richness.
>
> The weather is quite warm and the trees are putting forth their leaves and blossoms, presenting a pleasing contrast to the backward country we have just left. We observed a great many *liquor shops* in every part of the city which are always open, night and day, Sunday and all times, and also other stores were open ready for trade which some of the inhabitants said were kept by Jews but we came to the conclusion that there were some Gentiles amongst them.

The next day Charles Gould "called upon Mrs. Sharp and the Messrs. Williams[4] and dined; the pleasant and kind treatment of whom I shall always remember." Meanwhile, passage to St. Louis was secured on the steamer *Griffin Yeatman,* a vessel built in Cincinnati in 1847 and named for a prominent citizen who had engaged in boat building and other enterprises in that city for more than half a century.[5] According to the New Orleans *Daily*

---

[4] Friends of the Gould family at Newton.

[5] The Punch Bowl, a restaurant in present-day Cincinnati, was Yeatman's eating house, famous both because of its good food and because no one was refused service if he could not pay. Griffin Yeatman died in March, 1849; and at about the time the Boston-Newton party was in the city he was

Picayune, July 8, 1849, the *Griffin Yeatman* was a "magnificent, swift running light draught passenger steamer," having "fine accommodations." Captain Frederick Way, Jr., described her as "a large, light draft, low water packet," which "operated when many of the heavier boats were tied up."[6]

On this same day, Monday, April 23, David Staples reported:

> We also bought two waggons[7] for our trip across the plains having sattisfied ourselves we could transport more goods with the same number of mules than we could if we packed mules. Having got all our baggage on board the Steamer and all being redy we left at 7 P.M. and moved off down the river.

Charles Gould's account of their departure is more detailed.

> . . . We left Cincinnati at sunset. The weather was quite warm and slight rain falling. The boat was filled with passengers, every state room being occupied except the Captain's, which was politely tendered to us for our private use. Amongst the passengers was a noted bank robber in the charge of an officer, bound for St. Louis. We here saw a specimen of western life on boats for the first time; there was a set of gamblers seated around a table well supplied with liquor and keeping up their games until late in the night.
>
> April 24
>
> We waked up this morning and found ourselves quietly and steadily passing down the Ohio with the beautiful scenery upon the banks which makes the travelling upon this

---

eulogized by the Rev. Henry Jewell in a discourse titled "The Perfect Man" (Cincinnati *Daily Commercial,* April 23, 1849), later published as a brochure.

[6] Letter from Captain Way to the author, 1950. Captain Way is a noted authority on river boats.

[7] Usually wagons shipped by boat were left unassembled. Each piece was numbered and there was an accompanying chart of printed instructions for reassembling. The canvas tops came ready to slip over the wooden bows which held the cover in place.

river so interesting. Upon our right bank lies Indiana, on the left Kentucky. We reached Louisville at 10 o'clock, where we were oblidged to wait until 4 on account of the difficulty of getting through the lock. The river falls considerably opposite Louisville and it is necessary to lock the boats through the falls.

Louisville is very pleasantly situated upon the left bank of the river and stands up at quite a respectable height. Like all of the western cities, it is very regularly laid out, with wide streets and good looking houses, but the streets are quite filthy. The water tastes horribly, not one of our company being able to drink any at dinner. We saw the Kentucky Giant named Porter, who is 7 feet 8 inches in height. He keeps a liquor shop at the locks.

It was a day that Staples also enjoyed: "This morning was delightful and a New England[er] feels a peculiar sattisfaction on moving down such a river as the Ohio. . . . We had a good table set on the boat and a verry fine Captain."[8] And he, too, was impressed with the Kentucky Giant—"he has a fowling piece 10 ft in length and such a cane—He is quite feble now." In point of fact, Porter was then about forty years old. His cane, resembling a spiral bed post, measured four and one-half feet, and his rifle was eight feet long. Visiting his tavern could not have caused any embarrassment to the teetotalling New Englanders, for the Kentucky Giant also was an abstainer. Among other wonders at the tavern on the lock was the five-foot sword made and presented to him by a Springfield, Massachusetts, firm, which hung on the wall alongside a picture of his eighteen-room house where he lived with his mother.[9]

---

[8] Captain Cunningham brought the *Griffin Yeatman* into Cincinnati and, so far as can be determined, took the boat on to St. Louis. Sources: 1849 newspapers of Cincinnati, Louisville, Kentucky, and Cairo, Illinois.

[9] See "Jim Porter, the Gentlemanly Giant of Shippingport," a feature story by Melville O. Briney, Louisville *Times*, November 1, 1951. Charles

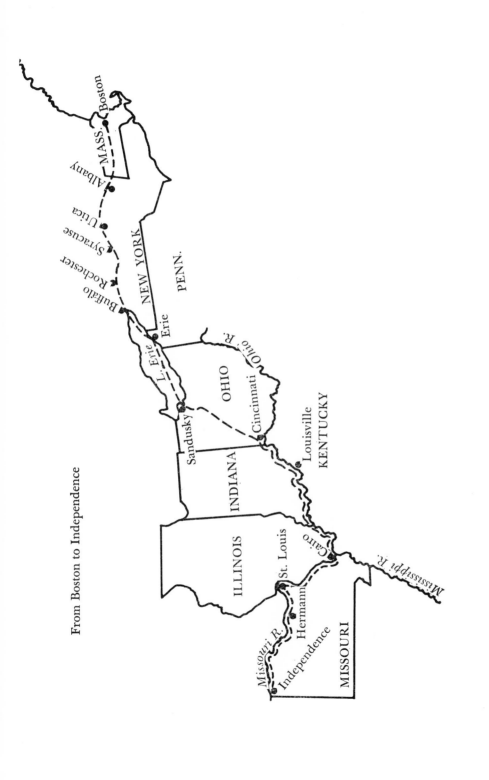

From Boston to Independence

April 25

We still continue on our way down the Ohio [wrote Gould], which loses none of its interest as we proceed. The beautiful level land upon either side partly cleared presents to one so fresh from New England as we are great contrasts from the barren and sterile rocks and hills of home. Last evening as we were passing through the locks we were much amused with the songs and dancing of some slaves occupied upon the locks, who accompanied their amusement with the real negro touch, much to the amusement of everyone on board.

In an entry carrying the same date, Staples noted that they arrived at the mouth of the Ohio at 10 A.M., touching at Cairo. "The vilages west and south look as though they lacked New England enterprise. No prety fenses round their houses, and they lack a finish so it looks to me." At Cairo, as at Cincinnati and Louisville, the newspapers announced the arrival of the boat, "and also a company of 125 [*sic*] persons, bound for California, called the Boston-Newton Joint Stock Association."[10]

Apparently the New Englanders' abstention from strong drink had become the talk of the boat, for shortly after the steamer left Cairo, as it entered the Mississippi, they were approached by an elderly man with thick, white hair and a long white beard reaching to his waist. "Now, boys," he said, "you must drink whiskey, or this water will kill you." The young men held a hasty conference, after which Albion Sweetzer, a confirmed prohibitionist, stepped out from the group and led his companions in a unanimous response. Their right hands raised above their heads, they solemnly declared: "Then we will die!"[11]

Dickens' visit to the Shippingport Goliath is recorded in his *American Notes* (1842); Dickens described Porter as "like a lighthouse walking among lamp-posts." Giant Jim died on April 25, 1859.

[10] *Daily Missouri Republican*, April 28, 1849, p. 3.

[11] This story as told by Sweetzer appears in Thompson and West, *History of Sacramento County, California, 1880* (Oakland, Calif., 1880), p. 292.

II

The next phase of their journey would take the Boston-Newton company up the Mississippi to St. Louis, already an old town in 1804 when it came under American sovereignty, and during the early decades of the nineteenth century the headquarters for the western fur trade and an outfitting place for much of the trade with Santa Fé. In the 1840's it was enjoying a period of spectacular growth; in fact, the population more than quadrupled, jumping from 16,469 in 1840 to 77,860 in 1850.

We entered the Mississippi River this morning [Gould wrote on April 26], but being quite unwell I could not witness the scenery very much. But I saw enough to see considerable contrast from the Ohio. The current runs very strong, about six miles an hour, which makes the progress of the boat very slow. I have been confined to my bed today, owing to my stomach becoming foul and disordered, but by taking emetic, I found myself relieved.

April 27

I found myself upon awaking a great deal better than I was yesterday and I feel in hopes of going on without any more drawbacks. What I feel most in want of is good, cool, fresh water, which it is impossible to obtain here. The waters of the river are dreadful muddy. The scenery is not as grand as it is on the Ohio; the banks not being so high do not form so bold and prominent outlines. *Carlo* [a dog] fell overboard this morning and David and Fred [Staples] have gone ashore to go back in search of him. The right bank of the river has changed its appearance, having grown more and more rocky, and in many places it presents a precipitous face to the river and forming high bluffs, while the left or Illinois side is perfectly level. We arrived at the long looked for city of St. Louis just as the sun was setting. The first object that attracts the attention of the traveller upon landing is the great number of steamboats that lie crowded together for half a mile or more at the landing. Thermometer 90° in the shade aboard the boat.

April 28

We staid on board [the *Griffin Yeatman*] last night and breakfasted here this morning. A bargain was made with the captain of the Bay State to take us up to St. Joseph for 8 dollars apiece. The committee are now out making the necessary purchases. Everything is all confusion. I have had no chance to examine the city, but from the view obtained from the river it has quite a pretty and businesslike appearance and will undoubtedly become one of the first cities in the union for wealth and population, but it is very muddy. We did not start out this morning as we expected. There are a great many passengers aboard, principally bound for California.

Those members of the company who did go ashore clearly made a favorable impression, for one of the St. Louis papers reported: "No finer looking or nobler set of men have yet passed this way, and their conduct since they have been in our city proves them to be men of the true grit for an enterprise like this, every one of them being a strict follower of the soundest laws of temperance."[12]

In the early morning hours of April 29, David Staples and his brother reached St. Louis and rejoined the party. For the story of what had befallen them we go back to pick up David's account, beginning on April 26, when the steamer entered the Mississippi.

[12] Quoted in an article, "Another 49er Gone," in the Newton (Mass.) *Graphic*, November 27, 1896, reporting the death of Benjamin Burt on October 14, 1896, in San Jose, California. It is apparent from the article that the editor had access to letters written by Burt to his family during the 1849 trek. A copy of the article was sent to Burt's daughter Clara, who pasted it in her journal. The Burt Journal is now in the Bancroft Library.

. . . This afternoon we saw a large island covered with wild geese. All the rifles on board were soon in requisition but to no purpose as we did not come near enough. The men on board seemed to enjoy murdering the ducks as passed near a *cove*.

April 27

This morning by the recommendation of our Dr quite a number of us went down to the Wheel house for the purpose of getting a shower Bath from the spray of the wheel. It was a good ideas as was prooved by our feelings during the day. After While I passed in the Wheel house. Brother Fred's dog *Carlo* thinking (to all appearance) I had gone overboard jumped over and was soon far in the rear. We saw him head for the shore and Brother Fred and I got set on shore to go back and search for him. This was 7 miles below St. Mary's Landing on the Missouri side. We started through the timbered bottoms. We searched in vain for him. It was accessive hot and having nothing to eat it was a luxury to find a log cabin where we got a little corn bread and butter-milk. After eating a lunch we started up the banks of the river for the landing. In the bottom lands water stands in little pools and on pasing through the Mosquitoes would arris in swarms and commence their work of drawing blod in hot haste. They were as bad as some of the Dr's in times past. We hailed two steamboats in the afternoon. They were New Orleans boats and asked us 5 dolls to take us up to St. Louis.

It was only 60 miles and our fare from Cincinnati to that place was only $4. We concluded to stay in the landing and take a smaler boat. We put up at a tavern such as is common out here and had another opportunity to observe western manners.

April 28

We took passage up the river in the *Oriental*, an infirm boat, at $3. and arrived in St. Louis at 4 A.M. on the 29.

54

At light we went in serch of our party. We found them on board the steamer Bay State and nearly ready to move up the river to Independence. Here [St. Louis] they bought the provisions for our overland consumption and hurried on, on account of the report that the cholera being quite prevelent. There was four cases on the boat that arrived the day before. St. Louis is a large place and destined to be the great point for emigrants to start from. Here they can purchase provisions cheap and a general outfit for a good deal less money than at Independence. . . .

The *Bay State* was a side-wheeler of 210 tons, built in Cincinnati in 1848. There were few conventional docks along the Missouri, but freight and passenger services were available to towns located where a boat could get in close enough to allow the gangplank, which was hinged to the boat and held in place by a boom, to be lowered to the riverbank. Stops also were made to pick up wood, which was stacked along the bank at designated places. The steamboat captain would leave a receipt for the wood he had taken. If, as occasionally happened, the pile had not been replenished, members of the crew gathered a supply, sometimes helped out by the passengers.

The *Bay State* left for St. Joseph at ten in the evening of April 29. Charles Gould's entry for that date reads:

> We staid aboard last night and 2 of our company were relieved of what money they had in their pockets, Mr. Evans having about $60 and Mr. Burt 2 or 3 dollars. The scoundrel made off as soon as he found there was an alarm given. There are a great many suspicious looking characters aboard and it requires our utmost vigilance to keep our things right. There is a company aboard from Boston called the Granite State Co. numbering 29 members.[13]

---

[13] The Granite State and California Mining and Trading Company, which was organized in New Hampshire, left Boston on April 17, 1849, the day after the departure of the Boston-Newton company. Its story is told by

We got under way a few minutes before 10 P.M. and proceeded up the Mississippi until we came to the Missouri and pursued up this for St. Joseph. The Missouri is very difficult to navigate owing [to the] channel becoming filled with sand. The waters are very muddy and new islands are constantly forming and old ones being carried away. There were religious services on board this afternoon—preaching by Rev. Mr. Haines of Boston.[14]

In Staples' journal, the Reverend Haines is further identified as being the minister with the Granite State company: "We invited him to preach and it was a pleasant sight to me to se me[n] from all parts of the Union come to gather in the Cabin and worship alike one *God*." On Monday, April 30, Staples wrote: "Today we have moved on well, occasionally getting aground on the shoales. This river is full of these places and requires the best of pilots to get a large boat up to St. Joseph, the destination of our boat." According to Gould's entry for the same day:

We stopped at a small German town called Harmon [Hermann] which is situated amongst high bluffs on the right bank of the river.[15] The sand blows so much in some places

---

Kimball Webster, a member of the party, in *The Gold Seekers of '49: A Personal Narrative of the Overland Trail and Adventures in California and Oregon from 1849 to 1854.* (Manchester, N.H.: Standard Book Co., 1917).

[14] Benjamin Burt wrote: "As we were obliged to travel on the Sabbath up the Missouri we had preaching by a Calvinist. This was the first Sabbath on which we travelled and it will be the last one. We shall keep the Sabbath as we would at home in New England." Letter of May 7, 1849, quoted in the Newton *Graphic*, November 27, 1896 (see note 12, above). The Reverend Haines (also spelled Haynes) settled in Sacramento, where he established a hospital in February, 1850.

[15] According to a letter of October 10, 1960, from Anna Hesse of Hermann, Missouri: "Hermann was settled in 1836 as a German Colony . . . among the bluffs on the right bank of the river. The name of the town as the pronounciation of the German people sounded to [Gould], he might well have written Harmon." She noted that the steamboats often traveled by night going upstream, but never did so going downstream.

as almost to obscure the view of distant objects. No occurence of particular interest has happened today.

May 1

Some of the company stepped ashore this morning and gathered some May flowers.[16] The gamblers kept up their game all night and it is said that one of them lost about $150. He is very tall, measuring about 6 ft. 5 in. in height, and very slim, and he looks old enough to know better. Today several of the *Kennebec fellows* together with some others are pretty well *smashed*. There has been quite an exciting race between this boat and the *Alton*, which is behind us and we think will be oblidged to stay there. There was quite a heavy thunder storm in the evening which caused so much darkness as to prevent the boat from running during the night.

Staples had no comment on the gamblers, but he noted that

We have learned there is a great difference between the Captain of this boat and the Captain of the *Griffin Yeatman*. This one is a real half cent Yankee. We live verry plain but healthy. The banks of the river look more ruged than the Ohio. The water is very Mudy but quite sweet. We observed quite a number of natural chimneys, ricks [rocks?] piled up as though the hand of man had been opperating on them. Nature works out some queer shapes. We got aground several times but got off without trouble.

Gould's account resumes on May 2:

The morning is clear and pleasant and we continue to glide on our way as smoothly as could be wished for. Early this morning we passed a small but beautiful *praire* which looked rich enough to last for ages without renewing. We here got a supply of milk, which makes quite a luxury for us

---

[16] Between the pages of Gould's diary there is still the imprint of a mayflower and the pressed flower itself.

and certainly has a much better effect on us than some other kind of *drink* have upon some of our *fellow passengers*. The company are now holding a meeting upon the hurricane deck to take into consideration the propriety of stopping at Independence.

The party was disturbed by the reports of the crowded conditions at St. Joseph. On April 21, 1849, the Independence *Expositor* had stated: "At St. Joseph there are now as many Emigrants as the Ferry will be able to cross, from now until the 1st of July, they having but one flat[boat] and making but two trips a day." It was also reported that three thousand emigrants had arrived up to April 25, and that roads in every direction were lined with wagons.[17]

It would save a good many miles of wagon travel if the Boston-Newton party went on to St. Joseph, but this advantage was outweighed by the prospect of weeks of delay at the ferry crossing. Consequently, it was decided at the meeting to change their plans and disembark at Independence.

---

[17] *Publications of the Nebraska State Historical Society*, XX (1922), 191. A May 12 report said that even with two steamboats assisting and with the two ferry boats running all day and most of the night, it was still impossible to handle the crowd of emigrants at St. Joe.

CHAPTER 5

Camp Grove

Independence, located where the Missouri River turns northward, had been an outfitting point for westward-bound wagon trains for more than two decades when the Boston-Newton company arrived there. Originally, after the opening of the Santa Fé trade, the town of Franklin (on the Missouri opposite present-day Boonville), was the starting point for trading caravans westward. However, according to Josiah Gregg in an account published in 1844,

> as the navigation of the Missouri River had considerably advanced towards the year 1831, and the advantages of some point of debarkation nearer the western frontier were very evident, whereby upwards of a hundred miles of troublesome land-carriage over unimproved and often miry roads might be avoided, the new town of Independence [founded in 1827], but twelve miles from the Indian border and two or three south of the Missouri River, being the most eligible point, soon began to take the lead as a place of debarkation, outfit, and departure, which in spite of all opposition it has ever since maintained. It is to this beautiful spot, already grown up to be a thriving town, that the prairie adventurer, whether in search of wealth, health, or amusement, is latterly in the habit of repairing about the first of May, as the caravans usually set out some time during that month. Here they

purchase their provisions for the road, and many of their mules, oxen, and even some of their wagons—in short, load all their vehicles and make their final preparations for a long journey across the prairie wilderness.

As Independence is a point of convenient access (the Missouri River being navigable at all times from March till November), it has become the general port of embarkation for every part of the great western and northern "prairie ocean." Besides the Santa Fé caravans, most of the Rocky Mountain traders and trappers, as well as emigrants to Oregon, take this town in their route. During the season of departure, therefore, it is a place of much bustle and active business.[1]

Independence boasted a brick courthouse, built in 1836, and a log-cabin schoolhouse where children studied the three R's to the sound of covered wagons rolling by—five hundred a day in May and June of 1849. The main street was lined with hotels, saloons, eating places, and a variety of shops. In May, 1846, a traveler had described the scene this way:

Teams thronged the highways; troops of men, women, and children hurried nervously about, seeking information and replenishing supplies. Jobbers on the street were crying their wares, anxious to sell anything and everything required, from a shoestring to a complete outfit for a four months' journey across the plains. Beads of sweat clung to the merchants' faces as they rushed to and fro, filling orders. Brawny blacksmiths with breasts bared and sleeves rolled high, hammered and twisted red hot metal into the divers forms necessary to repair yokes and wagons.[2]

[1] Josiah Gregg, *The Commerce of the Prairies,* ed. Milo Milton Quaife (Lincoln: University of Nebraska Press, 1967), pp. 19–21.

[2] Eliza Donner Houghton, *The Expedition of the Donner Party and Its Tragic Fate,* quoted in Julia Cooley Altrocchi, *The Old California Trail* (Caldwell, Idaho: Caxton Printers, 1945), p. 43.

The first journal entries of Charles Gould and David Staples in Independence are dated May 3. Gould wrote:

> We landed at Independence at 1 o'clock this morning [Staples says two o'clock] and succeeded in getting our goods landed at sunrise, except a part that could not be got at, so Mr. Sweetser went with them to St. Joseph to fetch them back. We pitched our tents this evening and we all being very tired, we slept very sound. The town of Independence is about 3½ miles from the steamboat landing upon a very pleasant situation and presents a remarkable business appearance.

Staples, who went with the other directors up to the town "to make some inquiries about matters," described Independence as having "the appearance of haveing grown up in one night like 'Jonah's gourd.' "

Benjamin Burt wrote his family that as near as he could tell

> there are about 5000 emigrants here, and 10,000 at St. Joseph's. Some who have been here quite a long time, have wasted their money in drinking and gambling and will return. . . . We find the gold fever is on the increase as we go West. From three-fourths to seven-eights of those on the route are temperance, steady men; ministers, doctors, and all classes of respectable citizens.[3]

The party chose a campsite, which they christened "Camp Grove," about a mile below Independence on a small stream. Here for the next ten days the men were busy with all the details of outfitting for the trail, and here for the first time they had a taste of living under canvas.

[3] Letter of May 7, 1849, quoted in the Newton *Graphic*, November 27, 1896. On May 17, 1849, the *Daily Missouri Republican* reported: "At least 14,000 persons have arrived at their various rendezvous and are ready, or have moved, for the plains." Quoted in *Publications of Nebraska State Historical Society*, XX (1922), 191.

One of the first matters to settle was the kind and amount of foodstuffs to purchase. The Boston-Newton party decided on three hundred pounds per person.[4] In the main, the food purchased consisted of flour, rice, beans, salt, tea, coffee, sugar, raisins, dried apples, jam, shortening, and smoked and salted meats.

A more difficult and time-consuming task was buying mules. Two kinds of mules were on the market:[5] American, coming mostly from Mississippi, Louisiana, and Arkansas, and Mexican (referred to in the journals as Spanish), coming from Texas. The latter were wild little creatures, much smaller than the American mules. Bred in an arid region, they could go long stretches without water and were generally favored for the long journey. Breaking them in, however, was no job for a novice, and it was fortunate for the Boston-Newton company that there were Mexicans available to hire as mulebreakers.

In addition to fitting harness to the mules and getting them shod, there was work to be done on the wagons. In 1849, most of the wagons on the market retained the lines of the familiar Conestoga wagon, but were smaller. Blue bodies and red wheels had been the style for more than a decade, and the patriotic color scheme was completed by the white canvas tops on which it was customary to paint the name of the company and the town and state from which it hailed. Companies which were well organized and well financed invariably had good-looking equipment, but by no means all the wagons that set out on the trail in 1849 were painted or embellished with fancy designs on their canvas covers.

Charles Gould's diary gives us an over-all view of the party's activities during their stay at Camp Grove.

[4] Newton *Graphic*, November 27, 1896.

[5] As of March 20, 1849, mules were selling at $50 to $55 per head and oxen at $45 to $50 a yoke. On April 29 it was reported that the supply of both exceeded the demand at Independence. *Publications of the Nebraska State Historical Society*, XX (1922), 189–190.

May 4

When we awoke this morning it was raining quite hard, making it very unpleasant for our first attempt at camping.

But, however, by putting on our rubber clothes, we got our marquee pitched and our goods under cover. If our friends should look in upon us we think that they would laugh at our awkward appearance. Every one of us being *green*, we go to work in a manner that would not come up to strict military tactics.

May 5

As we are getting more accustomed to camping, the better we like it. The Mt. Washington Co. arrived today.[6] The Star Co. also arrived, one of their company having the Cholera. The directors are in town making purchases of mules. The weather is quite warm although the sky is clouded. Mr. Dickenson arrived today.[7] The directors had quite an exciting scene in getting the 5 mules which they purchased home.

May 6

It rains this morning. I went with 8 others to help lead 3 mules into camp which had been purchased yesterday, and although we got along much better than we anticipated, yet the scene we presented was rather ludicrous. Mr. Sweetser arrived from St. Joseph with the remainder of the goods which had been sent there. Mr. [H. B.] Crist, whom we had fallen in with on our journey here, also came from the same place in consequence of the defalcation of the mule agent of his Company.

6 The Mount Washington Mining Company, organized in Boston, made plans to travel across the plains with the Granite State company.

7 It will be recalled that Harvey Dickinson, one of the directors of the company, had remained in Boston to take care of some business matters.

May 7

I have been to work in company with Mr. Ayers upon a wagon top for our small spring wagon. The directors purchased about 30 Mexican mules and 1 horse.

Gould and Ayer equipped their spring wagon with a stretcher so that, if necessary, it could be used as an ambulance. The stretcher consisted of a sacking made from a perforated elastic compound which could be supported by elastic springs that were suspended on a frame of wood or metal. Invented by Charles Goodyear, this type of stretcher was first used in the Mexican War.

May 8

Worked with Ayers part of the day upon the wagon top. Saw a case of Cholera in town.[8] Mr. Sweetser got thrown from a mule and got his wrist put out of joint. Mr. Dickenson and Felch purchased a quantity of corn.

May 9

There are 4 Mexicans in camp today engaged in breaking in the mules. They are black, miserable looking fellows, but seem to understand their profession.

May 10

The Mexicans are here again today breaking the mules. Messrs. Hough and Staples returned from an exploring expedition with 4 horses. It was voted by the company that we should unite with trains of Gen. Bodfish and Dr. Ormsby and also that we were willing to come under the military control of Gen. Bodfish in travelling across the country.[9]

[8] At this time the papers were reporting cholera at Independence and Kansas (three miles from Westport). There were thirty-five deaths on the steamer *Mary* and seven or eight on the *Kansas*. Another steamer, the *Monroe*, was "laid up and nearly if not quite deserted by the passengers, officers, and crew." *Publications of the Nebraska State Historical Society*, XX (1922), 191.

[9] In an initialed entry in his journal, dated 1911, Gould wrote: "For some

CAMP GROVE *(May 3–May 14)*

As the organization of the company proceeded, Gould, George Winslow, Harry Noyes, Benjamin Evans, and Lewis K. Whittier were designated as teamsters and the teams and equipment were drawn by lot.

May 11

The teams were divided by lot and the light spring wagon together with the best harness fell to my lot. I also selected my mules and harnessed 2 of them and drove them around.

Staples and Hough have gone off again. It was voted to receive Mr. Crist into our company by his paying into the funds of the company the regular sum, deducting the travelling expenses from Boston here.

May 12

I have been to work in putting my wagon in thorough repair. Mr. Whittier's team started off for the plains in good shape.[10]

Gen. Bodfish also started off, but had the misfortune to break one of his wheels when about 8 miles out, which will detain him for some time. . . .

May 13

The nights are quite cold but the days are quite warm. This morning is very beautiful.

May 14

There was a very heavy shower in the morning. Harnessed my team and drove it to town and back again. Did not start upon the journey as was expected.

---

reason, I do not remember, we did not finally join with Bodfish and Ormsby." Bodfish, who was a colonel, not a general, later served in the Civil War. In the early 1870's he explored a gold strike in Kern County, California, and the townsite was named after him. The sign directing the traveler to Bodfish was an old road through the Mojave Desert area leading into Bakersfield.

[10] Whittier started off ahead of the others to pick a "trial camp." See Chapter 6.

David Staples' journal for this period is largely devoted to the problems attendant on buying mules. After an initial purchase of three mules on May 4, he noted the next day that "the directors are at loss to know what kind of mules to purchase. Today we purchased 7 American mules but think [we] shall generally buy Spanish mules." On Sunday, May 6, after a three-mile trip with two companions to secure a pair of the beasts, he wrote rather plaintively: "No one knowes how vexatious it is to manage wild mules. These were as wild as *Arabs* and we were tired enough." On Monday he reported the purchase of thirty Spanish mules, "and at night our camp began to look like starting. But to new beginers, business crowds in every form. Waggons to buy, harnesses to fit, &c &c."

It was customary among organized groups for the doctor and officers of the company to ride horses, and buying them was another duty that Staples saw to.

May 8

Mr. Hough and I started in the country to purchase a few horses and chains, it being next to impossible to get any blacksmithing done. We directed our course to the town of Liberty, Clay County, Mo. We bought a verry fast horse for 55 dolls such as would bring in Mass $200, quick. The land here is a good deal prara and most of the horses raised on them [the prairies] will skim over the ground like a bird. We put [up] at a fine tavern and receved the best of treatment.

May 9

Friend Hough and I started out in the country to find a few horses. The day was a fine one and we enjoyed the ride much. We purchased 3 horses at an average price of 40 dolls. Here we bought our chains and whiffle trees as well as shoes for our mules, packed our chains on a mule and started for camp. We arrived late at home on account of being detained late at the ferry. All well in our party but they are dying with cholera all around us.

Perhaps the most interesting account of the stay at Camp Grove is that written by George Winslow to his wife, Eliza.[11] It is particularly valuable for the insight it gives us into the mind and the heart of this young man, typical of many, on the eve of venturing out into the limitless "prairie ocean." The Edward he refers to is his three-year-old son, George Edward. Another son, Henry, was born on May 16, four days after Winslow sat down to begin this letter.

Letter No. 3. Direct your letters to Sutters Fort, California.
Independence, May 12, 1849

My Dear Wife

I have purposely delayed writing to you until now so that I might be enabled to inform you with some degree of certanity of our progress and prospects; after starting for this State we heard so many Stories that I could with no certanity make up my mind wether we should suceed in getting farther than here and of course felt unwilling to mail too many letters as we neared this Town lest we might return *before* they did. I am happy to say that I heard from you today. Uncle Jesse [Winslow] and Brackett [Lord] were gratified by their wifes in the same maner. I am glad to hear that you are well. My health was never better than now.

You ask me to tell you what they say out here about the route. Well, those who have travelled it say we need borrow no trouble about forage; that *Millions* of Buffaloes have feasted on the vast praries for ages and now they have considerably dimmished by reason of the hunters &c. It is absurd to suppose that a few thousand emigrants cannot

[11] The letter is printed in George W. Hansen, "A Tragedy of the Oregon Trail," *Nebraska State Historical Society Collections*, XVII (1913), 110–126. The original of the letter is in the NSHS archives, presented to the Society by Carlton H. Winslow, a grandson of George Winslow.

cross. I have conversed with Col. Gilpin, a Gentleman who lives near by, upon the subject, and who has crossed to the Pacific five times; and his testimony is as above. We all feel very much encouraged and everybody says there is not a company in town better fitted out than ours. We have bought 40 mules and 6 horses and will have two more horses by monday. Our mules average us $52 each. We have also 4 waggons and perhaps may buy another. One of our waggons [Whittier's] left Camp today for the plaines 10 miles from here to recruit up before starting. We shall probably get underway next Tuesday or Wednesday. As to your 2nd question, vis. How I like to ride a mule. I would say that I have not ridden one enough to know and do not expect to at present as I have been appointed Teamster and had the good luck to draw the *best* waggon. We have covered it today in tall shape: the top has two thicknesses of covering so that it will be first rate in rainy weather or very warm weather, also to sleep in nights. As to "camping," I never slept sounder in my life—I always find myself in the morning—or my *bed* rather, flat as a Pan Cake as the *darned* thing leaks just enough to land me on Terra Firma by morning—it saves the trouble of pressing out the wind, so who cares?[12] It is excellent to keep off dampness.

We *diet* on Salt Pork, Hard and Soft Bread, Beans, Rice, Tea, Hasty Pudding and Apple Sauce, also smoked pork and Ham. Being out in the Air we relish these dainties very much. My money holds out *very* well. After buying several articles in Boston and "eating" myself on the road part of the time, I have about $15 on hand out of $25 which I had on leaving home. I have lost nothing except that Glazed Cup which was worth but little. Uncle Jesse, [Charles] Gould

---

[12] In 1849 the air bed came out with a new feature. So that the bed would not have to be inflated by blowing in the tube or using a hand bellows, the inventor, Charles Goodyear, designed it to inflate as it was unrolled.

and [William] Nichols are talking in our tent so I will defer writing more until morning.

Sunday morning, May 13. This is a glorious morning, and having fed and curried my mules and Bathed myself and washed my clothes I can recommence writing to you. Elisa, I will number this Letter 3 as I have sent you 2 before, the 2d from Sanduskey. I wish you would adopt the same system, then we may know if we receive every letter. We arrived here Friday P.M. May 4. Pitched our tents, cooked and eat our supper and went to *Grass,* slept first rate, commenced the next day to get ready to move on. It being considerable of a job and the season backward we shall not get *fairly* started before [May] 15 or 16. The weather is now warm and the grass is growing finely. For two days we—or some mexicans that we engaged—have been busily employed breaking 10 mules. It was laughable to see the brutes perform. To harness them the Mex's tied their fore legs together and throwed them down. The fellows then got on them, rung their ears (which like a nigger's shin is the tenderest part). By that time they were docile enough to take the Harness. The animals in many respects resemble a sheep. They are very timid and when frightened will sometimes kick like thunder. They got 6 harnessed into a team when one of the leaders feeling a little *mulish* jumped right straight over the other one's back and one fellow offered to bet the liquor that he could ride an unbroken one he had bought. The bet was taken—but he no sooner mounted the (fool) mule than he landed on his hands and feet in a very undignified manner. A roar of laughter from the spectators was his reward.

After they are broken they are, of the two, more gentle than the Horse. I suppose by this time you have some idea of a Mule. We have formed a coalition with two other (small) companies (one of which Edward Jackson of Newton, Con.[13] belongs to). The other from Me. consisting of only 4 persons, one of which is Col. Boafish [Bodfish] whom we have selected for our military commander. He belonged to the New Eng. Regiment and fought under Gen. [Winfield] Scott in Mexico. I think he is a first rate man for the office—by this union we have two Doctors and a man of military experience.

We found Samuel Nicholson here. His co. will start the fore part of next week. There has been some sickness here, principally among the intemperate which is the case every where, you know. Our company is composed mostly of men who believe that God has laid down Laws that must be obeyed if we would enjoy health—and obeying those laws we are all in the *possession* of good health.

I see by your letter that you have the blues a little in your anxiety for my welfare. I think we had better not indulge such feelings. I confess I set the example. I do not worry about myself—then why should you for me—I do not discover in your letter any anxiety on your own account—then let us for the future look on the bright side of the subject and indulge no more in useless anxiety. It effects nothing and is almost universally the Bug Bear of the Imagination.

The reports of the Gold regions here are as encouraging as they were at M[as]s. Just imagine to yourself seeing me return with from $10,000 to $100,000. I suppose by this time I may congratulate you on possessing a Family circle without me, for you know we use to say it required three to make a circle and Edward always confirmed it by saying *"No."* I wish you would keep a sort of memorandum of kindnesses received. I shall write to Br. David today requesting him to make great exersion to send you money when needful. You will of course inform him when that time arrives. I do

13 Actually, Newton, Massachusetts.

not wonder that Gen. [Zachary] Taylor was opposed to writing long letters when on the Field. I am now writing at a low Box and am compelled to stoop to conquer. I offer this as an apology for not writing more to you now and writing so little to others. I wish you would preserve my letters, as they may be useful for future reference. Although we shall leave probably before your next letter arrives, I expect to get it as one of our company will not start till about the 23, but will overtake us as he will have no Baggage of importance. He is from Ohio. Lord and Uncle Jesse will write today. They are both up and dressed and go at it like men at a day's work. Hough and Staples Have just returned from buying horses. They have brought two with them. They are very beautiful. I should like to send one home to Father. We pay about $50 for them apiece. In Boston they would bring $150. Respects to all.

Yours truly
George Winslow

It is impossible to be precise about the number of mules and horses comprising the Boston-Newton outfit when they left Camp Grove. Each wagon was pulled by a six-mule hitch and the company started out with five wagons. However, as future entries in the journals will show, this number had grown to seven by the time they crossed the Kansas River, and two more mules were purchased along with the seventh wagon.[14] It would require forty-two mules to pull seven wagons, and most large companies had mules in reserve. As for horses, George Winslow in the long letter quoted in this chapter, notes that six have been purchased and they will have two more "by Monday." In a continuation of the letter, he adds that Hough and Staples have returned from

---

[14] In mid-May, 1849, a correspondent at Fort Kearny reported that the ratio of men and wagons was 3½ to 1 in the emigrant trains he had observed so far that season. *Publications of the Nebraska State Historical Society*, XX (1922), 194.

buying horses, bringing two with them. If, then, there were eight horses and if every man except the teamsters was mounted on either a horse or a mule, the company would have needed at least fifty-three mules. But it should be emphasized that there is nothing firm about this figure. Some of the men may have ridden with the teamsters—Gould notes that Robert Coffey rode with him the first two days; also, Albion Sweetzer in later years stated that the men walked most of the time.

It was an unwritten rule of trail travel that the president or captain—in this case, Brackett Lord—always rode ahead of the train. It was his duty to pick the camp site for the noon meal, or nooning, and for the evening camp. The position of the wagons in the train was rotated: the wagon that was first in line one day took the last position the next, and so on. A mounted man always rode at the end of the train in case the last wagon should have difficulties.

There is no definite information on how the work was parceled out to each man. Obviously, there would be the horses and mules to be looked after, and the harness and wagons to be kept in repair. The animals would have to be harnessed or saddled in the mornings, unharnessed or unsaddled at night, and picketed. Probably the teamsters took care of the animals that drew the wagons and the men who rode horses or mules took care of their mounts.

The need to stand guard at night was a source of contention in some companies, and some men refused the duty. Entries in the Gould journal indicate that there were two watches; at times Gould stood guard the first half of the night, and at other times the second half. So it seems that this work also was rotated, and this would necessitate some bookwork. If twenty of the men were available for guard duty, in a ten-day period each would have stood guard once for a half night. Since the time a man stood watch—the first or second half of the night—also would be rotated, it would be necessary to keep a written record. No doubt one of the officers other than the president—Felch, Osborn, or Jesse Winslow—would have looked after this matter.

The cook, George Thomason, would have been free from all duties other than those pertaining to food. He had helpers, but it is not known if the helpers were rotated. After giving consideration to this question, I believe that two permanent helpers would be the most efficient arrangement. The food and utensils had to be packed and loaded on a wagon in the morning; unloaded and reloaded at noon; and unloaded again at night. Water was needed at each camp, and sometimes it had to be carried a good distance. Also, wood was needed for fire. The more accustomed the cook's helpers were to taking care of these chores, the more quickly they would be able to carry them out. And since nothing was so dear to the heart of a man on the trail as food, it seems there would have been special concern over orderly management of these details.

CHAPTER 6

Independence to the Little Blue

On the first phase of the trip across the plains, California-bound emigrants headed out of Independence in a southwesterly direction. They traveled along the old Santa Fé Trail for about forty miles, parting company with it where a crudely lettered sign proclaimed ROAD TO OREGON. The Boston-Newton party followed the custom of halting for two or three days at a "trial camp" a few miles out from Independence in order to give the inexperienced men a chance to put in practice techniques of camping on the trail. Here, for example, the men were drilled in circling the wagons at nightfall for protection in case of an Indian raid, and were broken in to stand guard.

David Staples' report of the first two days at trial camp is extremely succinct.

May 14

From the 9th to the 14th was spent in preparing for the journey. All being ready we made a final move from Grove Camp, as we call it, at Independence. We moved out 13 miles where there was plenty of grass. The mules wild and roads mudy. It was hard for man and beast.

May 15

We lay by and arranged our loads, etc.

75

Charles Gould's journal gives a much fuller picture:

May 15

It rained heavily all last [night] with severe lightning and thunder. R. Coffey and myself slept in our wagon. After much delay we started off upon our long expected journey at 12 o'clock N. The heavy rains of last night had rendered the roads very muddy and unsafe. We found the roads almost impassable in places, sometimes going up steep hills and then again going down into deep gullies which almost shook the wagon to pieces. After proceding about 5 miles, we came to the Blue praire. It differed very much from my idea, it being a rolling instead of a level prairie; but it exceeded in beauty and richness anything I ever beheld.

We had proceded on our way without any particular event until about sunset, when we found ourselves stuck fast in the mud, from which we did not get extricated until after dark; and after wandering about for some time, we found the camp, it being about 11 P.M. when we got our team put up.

May 16

R. Coffey and myself slept in our wagon last night. It was decided that 6 mules should be sent back half way to Independence to get a loaded wagon left there by Noyes. Whittier and myself went and drove the team. We got into camp about dark. The situation of our camp is too wet to be very pleasant, although it has the advantage of a good supply of excellent water. The grass is about 6 inches high, giving our animals a good chance to graze. Mr. Noyes arrived in camp a few minutes after I did with a new wagon, thus giving us much relief, for our teams were too heavily loaded for expedition or success. There is a man in the tent next to us very sick with the cholera. They have called upon our M.D., theirs having deserted them.

Asiatic cholera, apparently brought to New Orleans by vessels from overseas, was carried up the Mississippi and Missouri rivers. On May 9, 1849, one traveler noted that a steamer arriving in St. Louis that day from New Orleans carried five hundred emigrants, forty-seven of whom had died of cholera en route.[1] The disease followed the forty-niners out onto the prairies and struck again and again between the western settlements and Fort Laramie.[2] The Mount Washington company lost five men to cholera between Independence and the Red Vermillion River, and by June 5, 1849, thirty-eight graves had been dug near the crossing of the Red Vermillion.[3] The dread disease was raging in many parts of the United States that summer, particularly in cities where travelers changed from one form of transportation to another, and it was also rampant in port cities of foreign countries.

May 17 was the last day in trial camp. On that day Charles Gould wrote:

[1] See Georgia Willis Read and Ruth Gaines, eds., *Gold Rush: The Journals . . . of J. Goldsborough Bruff, 1849–1851* (2 vols.; New York: Columbia University Press, 1944–1949), I, 439.

[2] Contemporaneous accounts differ about the number and location of deaths from cholera on the trail, but most agree that they occurred before the emigrants reached the mountains. In early June, 1849, one correspondent reported: "I hear of no epidemic among the emigrants beyond Ft. Kearny [in present Nebraska]. As near as I can learn, about 200 have died on the road from cholera." *Publications of the Nebraska State Historical Society*, XX, (1922), 205. Later in the month the correspondent signing himself "Joaquin" reported 58 marked graves between St. Joseph and Fort Laramie. The number of deaths from the Missouri River to that point was estimated at $1\frac{1}{2}$ per mile. *Ibid.*, 208, 209. This estimate also appears in a standard source, Leroy R. Hafen and C. C. Rister, *Western America* (New York: Prentice Hall, Inc., 1941), p. 357.

[3] But the Granite State company, with which the Mount Washington company was traveling, lost no men. See D. M. Potter, ed., *Trail to California* (New Haven: Yale University Press, 1945).

77

R. Coffey and myself were routed out at 3 A.M. in consequence of Messrs. Crist and Evans taking our wagon back for the purpose of having it mended and to get some more bread and other things.

All are busy today preparing for the journey, which is to commence in earnest. Some are repacking their wagons, others are training their mules. Some of the scenes presented in breaking the mules are exceedingly ludicrous. Sometimes one mounts the animal, 2 more have hold of his head and another goes ahead with a rope. The mule pulls back for awhile and then he springs to throw; but finding himself overpowered, he finally allows himself to be dragged along, only to renew his tricks when he can get a chance.

It is clear from David Staples' account that he was responsible for providing one of the ludicrous scenes:

May 17

Today we divided the rideing horses by lotery. They were all brought up and numbered, horses and mules, and as bad luck would have it I drew the smallest Spanish mule we had in the lot. It was a cream colored one. I riged on a Mexican sadle and trimmings and mounted. Being full six feet tall I must have presented a picture truly ridiculous. My feet came within less than a foot of the ground. He used his best endeavours to throw me off but failed. And many a hearty laugh the boys have had at my expense today.

My friend Hough was more unfortunate haveing been throwed several times from a similar article of horse flesh. . . .

From here on, the two accounts of the journey are paired under the date for the day, unless otherwise indicated. Charles Gould's entry appears first.

May 18

All hands are busy in preparing to resume our journey this morning, but owing to unavoidable delays we did not get started until about 12 N. For 2 or 3 miles the country had the same general appearance of that we had passed over since we came upon the praire. About 4 miles from our camp brought us to the little Blue Creek [of Missouri]. This is a small stream about 25 yds. wide, but it is quite difficult to cross owing to a sharp muddy pitch upon its opposite bank. We were stalled here and were obliged to partly unload our wagon to get through. After we had proceded about 2 miles farther, and while we were waiting for the rest of the teams to come up, my near forward mule took fright at a cow and calf that was passing and suddenly turning around started the rest of the teams, turning the wagon so suddenly around as to break the pole. The rest of the teams encamped about 1 mile ahead of us. We were obliged to stay where we were.

[Staples][4]

. . . We got ready and moved 7 miles over a very rough road and crossing quite a stream. Here the hard work comes for men lifting and prying out of the mud waggons. We camped on the edge of the prara and a fine sight it was, as far as the eye could reach nothing but roleing plane. During the day we had two poles (or toungs) broken by our mules being wild and teamers not acquainted with driving.

We camped tired and hungry.

May 19

R. Coffey and myself staid to keep guard over our wagon last night. We were so fortunate as to find a blacksmith and wheelright's shop within a mile ahead of us.

Our repairs were completed by noon and the whole company were on their way at 2 P.M. We entered upon a praire which was beautiful and rich beyond description. It differed from the praire that we passed before we came to

---

[4] This entry was a part of the May 17 entry, but clearly describes events of May 18. Similarly, the next Staples entry describes events of May 19 though it is dated May 18. There is no May 19 entry in the journal.

the Blue Creek, it being much more level and having no gullies, but still the swells rise quite high and the road seems to ascend quite fast as we proceed. The richness exceeds anything which I have ever seen, the whole appearance being that of a high cultivation. We reached a spring about dark where we encamped for the night.

Distance about 12 miles.

[Staples]

We spent the first part of the day in mending our waggons. We passed on 13 miles over the most beautifull country man ever beheld. Prara pinks were in abundance and the odor arrising from them delightful to one's allfactory's. One that has never seen these plains can form no idea of their vastness. It looked like an ocean of prara. Only one thing we observed to mar the scene. That was quite a number of new made graves, and the voluntary thought and wish was that he had laid up for himself treasure in heaven in seeking treasure across the plains and the thought naturally occur it may our lot next but large hope and stout hearts will do much towards sustaining us. We arrived in camp late. Found water but no wood. This will be our great trouble in passing over this woodless country.

Sunday, May 20

We resume our journey at 9 this morning.[5] The route continued over the same praire that we were on yesterday and the scene presented had the same rich and luxuriant appearance.

At 2 we reached a very small stream, on the banks of which were encamped the parties of Gen. Bodfish and Dr.

---

[5] Although the company originally intended to rest on the Sabbath, for the reasons David Staples gives in his entry for this date it was necessary to push onward.

Ormsby and E. Johnson, all of whom intend to accompany us on our journey.[6]

It rained quite hard for a short time before we left our camp, but after we had been encamped about 1 hour it began to rain again and it soon increased to one of the most powerful storms that ever I witnessed. Owing to the storm it was decided not to move until morning.

[Staples]

We felt it our duty to move today as we had no wood to cook with and poor water. We traveled some 12 miles to what is called Indian Creek. This is inhabited by the Shawnees.[7] Most of them have left their houses on the road on account of the Emigrants haveing the Cholera.

We saw one half breed, quite inteligent. He said, "Great many go never get there." Here we found wood and a fine spring. Here we found quite a number of emigrating parties.[8] Before we got onharnessed there camp up quite a shower, and such showers as they have on the prara beats all I ever saw. We put up our tents but were blessed with a soft bed by the ground being well soaked. This is one of the beauties of camp life.

---

[6] The fourth member of this party was Major William Ormsby, a brother of Dr. Ormsby. The brothers are mentioned in Evelyn Teal, *Flying Snowshoes* (Caldwell, Idaho: Caxton Printers, Ltd., 1957). The Ormsbys reached California shortly before the Boston-Newton party arrived at Sutter's Fort. Major Ormsby was killed in a fight with Indians at Pyramid Lake, Nevada, in 1860. (Information courtesy of Verla M. Stinson, Ormsby County Recorder, Carson City, Nevada.)

[7] The Shawnees, an eastern, Algonquian tribe, had gradually been forced westward to Kansas, where they had a reservation from 1825 until 1845, when a large part of the tribe moved on to Indian Territory, settling along the Canadian River.

[8] Emigrating parties commonly rendezvoused at Indian Creek and made arrangements to travel on together for the sake of greater security. The Boston-Newton company, however, decided to remain independent.

May 21

We got started this morning between 7 and 8, the other parties being in advance of us. Owing to the heavy rains of yesterday, the travelling was very severe and slow. The rich soil of the praire when wet by rains becomes very soft for 3 or 4 inches and causes the animals' feet to slip and the wheels to stick. We encamped at noon upon the border of a small stream about 4 miles from our encampment of last night. We continued on our way until near night, when we came to a small creek which was very difficult to cross. I succeeded in crossing with great difficulty with the help of oxen, but the rest of the teams not getting to the creek until dark, could not get through until morning, some of them getting stalled in the mud.

[Staples]

We got started at 8 o'clock as it is a great job to harness up wild mules. We stoped at noon, baited our mules on the banks of a fine creek. Moved on till six o'clock and camped, haveing had a hard day's work for our mules, it being muddy by last night's shower.

May 22

We left camp at 9, the rest of the teams having succeeded in crossing the creek. After travelling 3 or 4 miles over the praire, we came to the *Wakarusa* River, which is about 75 feet wide, the banks being so steep that it became necessary to attach oxen to the wagons to pull them out. The river bottom for about 1 mile is very heavy timbered and the trail horrible muddy, so that it became necessary to double the team to get them out. From timber to the high praire, a distance of about 2 miles, is a mirey marsh and proved the most difficult place to get our teams through that we have yet passed, the wheels in many places to their hubs. This marsh is covered with grass about 1 foot deep which seems to be a great haunt for snakes, two of which sprung upon our men, but very fortunately did not bite them. They are the Moccassin snake, very poisonous.

[Staples]

Today we crossed the Wakarusa River. The banks were steep. We had to let our wagons down by ropes and hired some Santa Fee oxen to get our teems up the opposite bank. There is heavy timber for a half mile on each side of the river. For three miles we had to pass over a wet bottom prara. Had to double teems and much of the way the wheels went down to the hub. However we have got through it at dark and camped on [a] fine rise on the high prara. Tonight for the first time our ears have been saluted by the howling of wolves about our camp.

May 23

There was a heavy thunder[shower] about sunrise this morning in consequence of which we did not start until 11 A.M. After proceeding 2 or 3 miles we rose by a circuitous road to some high table land, which is mostly surrounded with a stone wall,[9] which could be taken as a work of art, were it not for its extent. After traveling about 1 mile farther over a very good road, we camped for the night in consequence of the severe labor that our animals had been subjected to for the last 2 or 3 days. A good many praire hens were seen, but none were shot. Wolves were heard howling at a small swamp 1 mile distant. 2 of our men started for them, but did not succeed in shooting one. There was another heavy shower this evening.

[Staples]

Today we have traveled over a roling prara and as we passed along the ridge we could see where the streams were by the lines of wood.

[9] The stone wall is near the present town of Lawrence, Kansas.

The morning is clear and beautiful. The birds are singing, wolves are howling, and all hands are busy in preparing for the day's work. Breakfast soon being over and the mules harnassed, we were promptly on our way at 6½ A.M. The road being quite good, we accomplished the best day's work that we have since we commenced our journey. Our route continued over the same high, rich rolling praire as before. We travelled until nearly 6, when we encamped upon a beautiful slope of the praire near an excellent spring of water. Soon after we had encamped and had got our animals picketed out, a severe thunder storm broke upon us which exceeded everything in power and fury that I have ever witnessed. Everything was drenched with rain.

[Staples]

Today we made a good drive haveing traveled full 25 miles. We camped at a small stream at 5 oclock. Mr. Felch and I started out to hunt wolves we heard nearby. We saw them but could not get a shot at those fiends of the prara. They are a redish color and all the evening our camp has been kept awake by their howling. Today I have been taken with the diarea, common now on the prara, and have been kept quite busy attending to the wants of nature, having 25 passages today.

May 25

Owing to the heavy rain of last night, we did not start so early as usual. After travelling 2 or 3 miles we came to a creek, but the heavy rains had raised the water from 18 inches to 4 feet, in consequence of which we were obliged to unload our wagons and ferry the contents across in our India rubber boat, which took until night to accomplish. We were visited by several Indians today. They were all mounted upon beautiful fat horses, which they ride with great ease and skill. They are dressed mostly after the fashion of the

From Independence to the Little Blue

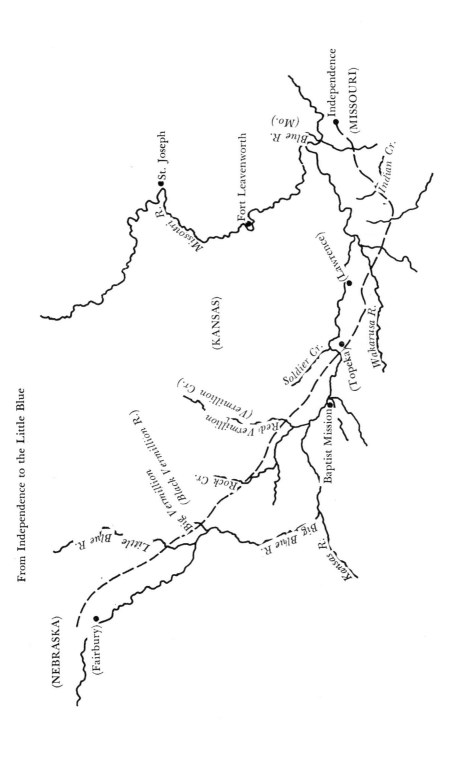

whites, some of them, however, having on some articles of Indian apparel. They seem quite anxious to trade horses.

[Staples]

Got an early start. At 11 o'clock we came to a small creek which was much swolen by the late rains. Here we had to unload our waggons and draw them across by ropes. We got our goods over in our rubber boat and found it to be valuable. We got all over at six o'clock and camped on the left bank. At sunset we were saluted by the screching of a dozen Indians who riding at full gallop towards our camp. They were *Potawatamas*[10] and only wanted wisky. We had none to give them and they went of[f] soon without giving us any trouble. Today I have been followed up with the diarea as hard as yesterday. It soon weakens one. I hope to be better tomorrow.

May 26

We started at 6 and 2 miles brought us to the lower ferry of the Kansas, but no ferryman could be found for two or three hours, when a half-breed accompanied by 4 Indians, came and commenced cleaning and repairing their boat, which took them several hours to accomplish, after which it was decided that the wind and current was too strong to attempt crossing today.[11] We have not gained but 5[?] miles in 8 days, but we trust in making it up in the future. The river is about 300 yds. wide where we crossed it. The waters are very muddy, the whole appearance being the same as the

[10] First encountered, in the seventeenth century, along the western shores of Lake Huron, the Potawatomis were an Algonquian tribe allied to the Chippewas and the Ottawas. They emigrated southward and, especially between 1836 and 1841, beyond the Mississippi to Kansas and western Iowa. These western, or Prairie, Potawatomis were given a reservation in Kansas in 1846.

[11] The Indians who repaired the boat were the Tappan brothers, who had French blood. One of their descendants was Charles Curtis, Vice President of the United States under President Herbert Hoover (1929–1933).

Missouri. I improved a chance to wash my clothes today so as to have everything in readiness for the future. It was very cold last night and has continued so through the greater part of the day.

[Staples]

Today we got started early and after an hour's travel came to the Kansas River. At the lower crosing here we had to be ferryed over in flat boats owned by half breeds. The wind blew and we could not persuade them to take us over till tomorrow. Several Indians have visited us today—all Friendly.

Sunday, May 27

The morning is clear and beautiful, the weather having moderated considerably since yesterday. The work of ferrying was commenced this morning at [?] and at [?] the whole was accomplished. The wagons are driven upon a flat-boat and poled across by Indians. There are a great many straggling Indians around, dressed in all varieties of style, some after the manner of the whites and some a mixture of White and Indian, others of the Indians. They all have a wretched appearance, with the exception of a Chief, who is dressed in thorough Indian style with a great variety of ornaments attached to his body. We proceded 5 miles farther when we found ourselves in the midst of an extensive marsh, which proved so bad that we crossed over onto an elevated ridge. This proved a very difficult job, but we finally accomplished it with great labor at 9 P.M.

[Staples]

This morning we got ferryed across at a cost of 10 cents a head for our animals and $1.00 for our waggons. We got all over at noon and passed out on a wet prara some six miles on to high land. We got into camp at 9 o'clock haveing to double our teems to get along. The last waggon had got in carralle [corral] when the mules took fright and broke a toung to our best wagon. This morning George Winslow

86

was taken with diarea and vomiting, this evening feels some better. At the crossing we met a party returning, haveing lost a husband, father, and Friend of Cholera. We bought a pr. of mules and a waggon of them. The mules we paid $200 pr pair and noble fellows they are to[o]. The great trouble to getting along is our loads are heavy for such bad roads. We saw a Cheif of the *Caw* nation.[12] He behaved with a great deal of dignity. He was full six feet tall, strait as an arrow head, shaved all but a top [k]not. He asked for coffey, tea, sugar &c. Our camp tonight is on a beautifull rise with a creek on our right and the Kansas on the left—a grand scene for a painter.

May 28

One of the poles of the wagon having got broken last night, we were obliged to stop this forenoon to repair it. We finally got started at 2 P.M. and travelled about 10 miles. Our road lead over a rolling praire of great beauty. Some of the views were of great beauty, presenting a rich treat to the eye of the traveller.

The Soldier Creek[13] lies upon our right and the Kansas upon our left. The road is rather hard owing to the ruts being deep and the ground being soft. We encamped at night near a spring of pretty good water.

[Staples]

This morning was spent in mending our waggon. We passed on till six o'clock over roling prara and camped near a good spring.

New species of flowers continue to attract our attention. Distance traveled 12 miles.

---

[12] The Kansa, or Kaw, Indians were a southwestern Siouan tribe most closely related to the Osages. They lived along the Kansas River and in 1846 took a reservation near the Council Grove. They were later removed to Indian Territory.

[13] Soldier Creek was bridged when the city of Topeka was laid out.

May 29

We got started this morning at 6 and made quite good time until we came to a small clear creek with steep banks which took us some time to cross. We had not got more than 3 or 4 miles from the creek when Geo. Winslow, who has been complaining for a few days, was suddenly taken violently sick with the Cholera, which threw us all into confusion and obliged us to camp where we are. It is not thought that Winslow will live until morning.

[Staples]

We got started early this morning. I feel better today and am in hopes to feel better still by being carefull what I eat. George [Winslow] is better owing to the attention of our Dr. [Dean Jewett Locke].

11 o'clock A.M. We are at Soldier Creek. The east bank of this stream is verry steep. We let our teems down by ropes and were fortunate in getting over in an hour. We drove out to grass through the timber and got some diner. George eat some of the minute puding. We moved on an hour and George was taken vomiting and cramp, the worst kind of a cholera attack. We stoped immediately. No water within a half mile or wood. We hope for the best in his case but fear the worst. This evening he is out of his head.

May 30

G. Winslow is still alive, but it is considered that he cannot long survive. D. E. Esterbrook is also quite sick. There seems to be a general complaint amongst the company of diarrhea. Messrs. Hough and Staples have got back to the Mission[14] to get some necessaries which are found to be wanting. We remain encamped yet where we were yesterday.

[14] There were three missions in the region that became Kansas Territory, each partly supported by the United States government. The mission operated by the Presbyterians was near Leavenworth, and the Methodist Mission was about twenty miles east of the Baptist Mission, the one referred

[Staples]

This morning George is some better but it is doubtfull if he lives. I watched with him last night. I am near sick in consequence. At 2 o'clock he went into a calaps state and it was with greatest exertion we succeeded in bringing him to. We all gave him up but he would not beleve he was near his end. We laid by today to give George quite [quiet] repose. This evening George is better and we have some hopes of his recovery. This afternoon Hough and I went back 10 miles to the Potawattoma tradeing post for some articles for the association. This is quite a town, some six or eight stores there filled with nearly everything wanted to eat, drink, or wear. While there a shower came up and we could not get across the river till dark, and then only by paying double price. We got in camp late.

May 31

Geo. Winslow is better and strong hopes are entertained for his recovery. Estabrook is also better[15] and there seems to be a much healthier feeling in the company. I busied myself in oiling my harness and in making things in proper shape to start again. We feel in hopes of being able to go a short distance tomorrow.

---

to here. Located on the south side of the Kansas River, it was founded by the Reverend Isaac McCoy, who had a long record of bringing education to the Indians. Although partly supported by government funds, the mission was under the direction of the Baptist Church. The natives were taught farming methods and the fundamentals of the English language. An extensive farm surrounded the buildings. The mission also served as an outfitting place for travelers. See Isaac McCoy, *History of Baptist Indian Missions* (Washington, D.C., 1840) and Isaac McCoy, *Periodical Account of Baptist Indian Missions within the Territory for . . . 1836* (Shawnee Mission, Kansas, 1837).

[15] Shortly after Easterbrook became ill, Milo J. Ayer took it upon himself to care for the lad, and a friendship was formed that was not to be broken until Ayer's death fifty years later.

[Staples]

Today our sick men are better. We still stay in camp so not to expose them. This afternoon four of us started for the Kansas with our sein[e] to fish. We tried but caught only one. We returned and I lost my revolver on my way to camp. Bad luck. Hope to find it in the morning.

June 1

The patients feeling much better, it was thought best to proceed as long as the strength of the patients would allow. We passed over a high rolling praire of great beauty with an excellent dry road. We encamped on the bank of a small stream bordered with a most beautiful growth of Oaks. It is called "Black Paint" or "Sandy Creek." The distance from the camp of last night about 16 miles.

[Staples]

George and Easterbrook are better this morning. I took an early start to serch for my pistol. After looking an hour I found it. Good luck. I picked a fine bunch of flowers and returned to camp well sattisfied. Today we made up beds in the waggons for our sick and moved on slowly. We encamped on a small creek. Plenty of wood. Distance traveled today 12 miles. Our men stand it well.

June 2

We commenced crossing the creek at 7 A.M. The banks were very steep and the bottom very soft and muddy, but we succeeded without any accident by doubling our teams. At a distance of 4 miles farther we came to Hurricane Creek, which was still worse than the last. We again doubled our teams and got them all hauled through by 3 P.M. This stream is also bordered by very handsome Oak timber. After we had got through the timber we came to a very soft marsh, about 1 mile in length, which proved very difficult to our teams and it occupied us some time in getting through, after which we came to the high rolling praire again, which presented some of the richest and most beautiful scenery that I ever saw. We encamped at an excellent spring 12 miles from our encampment of last night. This is the hardest day's work that we have yet had and all hands seem glad to get into camp.

[Staples]

Today the men are better. We have traveled over a roling prara with some of the most beautiful landscape views I ever saw. It looked as though some wealthy monarch of the East had spent a fortune in laying it out. Today we could not camp till late on account of not finding water and wood. We camped at sun set on the banks of a small stream. George is tired and quite sick. I am to watch with him tonight. Distance traveled today 16 miles.

Sunday, June 3

We started at 10 this morning and went about 12 miles.

Our route continued over the rolling praire as before and nothing of particular [interest] occurred except the breaking of a wagon pole. The sick remain about the same. The journey is not affecting them seriously.

[Staples]

We concluded to move on a short distance. George is not much better. It is hard to ride all day. We passed some verry bad places, lowered our waggons down the steep pitches. It is the most vexing life man ever led. Tonight while eating supper a German party came along and pasing a bad place over goes the waggon. Wheels broke all up. Men cross and tired. Distance traveled 15 miles. Just as we were coming into camp one of our toungs got broke, and so it goes.

June 4

We stopped this forenoon to put in a new pole, which was accomplished by noon, when we started and travelled until 5 P.M. I have got to watch with G. W[inslow] tonight.

The road has been very good today.

[Staples]

This morning was spent in mending our waggons. This afternoon we started on over roling prara with but little to relieve the monotony except a great number of plover and prara hens that start up at every rod. We camped today on a small stream at half past five. Distance traveled 10 miles.

June 5

We started at 6 this morning, all in good spirits. 5 miles brought us to the Big Vermillion.[16] The bank is so steep that it became necessary to lower the wagon down with ropes. The bottom is gravelly and the opposite bank quite easy to ascend. The creek is about 50 yds. wide and the water about 1 foot deep where we crossed. The bottom is timbered with Oak, Elm, Locust, &c. After leaving the river bottom we again entered upon the high rolling praire, such as we have heretofore passed over, only exceeding it in grandeur and scenery. 15 miles brought us to the Big Blue, which very fortunately for us was very low so that we found no difficulty in crossing. We found here many beautiful cold springs, which were a great luxury to us.[17] The Big Blue is about 100 yds. in width and in high water is not fordable. Some of our company caught some fish in the creek.

---

[16] There are two rivers in Kansas, a few miles apart, named Vermillion. The Red Vermillion, a branch of the Kansas River, is sometimes referred to as the Little Vermillion. The Black or Big Vermillion is a branch of the Big Blue.

[17] This was Wyeth Creek, now called Rock Creek. In 1832, the fur trader Nathaniel Wyeth of Boston and his New Englanders passed this way en route to the Rockies. Frémont and his scout Kit Carson were among those who carved their names in a red sandstone above the creek; they bivouacked there on June 22, 1842. In 1917, Charles Dawson of nearby Fairbury, Nebraska, cut the names of Frémont and Carson deeper into the stone. At that time, Dawson made a map of sections of the old trail through Jefferson County, Nebraska.

[Staples]

This morning we were all up for an early start. Most of our party indulge in bathing when they have a chance and this morning they looked like ducks dipping in the limpid stream. We passed the Big Vermillion before noon. Moved on at a rapid pace and arrived at the Big Blue at 4 o'clock. The stream was low and we were soon over. We camped just out of the timber near a fine spring that run a stream out of the bank of rock. There is a rich smell on this river resembles the odor of a strawberry bed. Here some of our party caught a pail full of fine fish. Distance traveled according to Fremont 25 miles.[18] George is still improving fast and with good roads will not retard our progress any. Esterbrook is got out about camp.

June 6

We got under way at 5 this morning. After leaving the river bottom you ascend upon the high bluffs which overlook the whole valley. The prospect here is very beautiful. Our route continues as usual over the high rolling praire. The road has been beautiful in many places, being as smooth and hard as a plank floor. About an hour before sunset a terrific thunder shower arose which baffles all description to describe. The lightning flashed, sometimes dazzling the eyes, and the thunder deafening the ears and the rain falling in torrents. It was altogether the grandest scene that ever I witnessed. When the rain ceased to fall, the sun had set and

---

[18] The reference is to a guidebook. In Note 5 to "The Journal of David Jackson Staples," edited by Harold F. Taggart, *California Historical Society Quarterly*, XXII, 2 (June, 1943), 147–148, it is stated that after 1845 emigrants usually carried a copy of Frémont's report of his 1842 and 1843–1844 expeditions and his map, which showed in great detail the overland route from Westport (present Kansas City, Missouri) to Fort Walla Walla, and which also provided information about water, fuel, forage, game, and Indians. The Frémont report "was the source for a number of pamphlets issued during the gold rush. . . . Staples undoubtedly carried one of these works as a guide."

darkness had closed in. My team had got 3 miles behind the head of the train. It was about 9 when I got into camp. We came about 20 miles today.

[Staples]

This morning our sick are still better. We got an early start, traveled 15 miles before noon. Came to a small creek of poor water but learned by one of Fremont's guides that near by there was a fine spring; we did not find it, not knowing where to look. We moved on till four when one pair of mules in the last teem gave out from hard driving. Mr. Wilson and I started back with an extra pair and a shower coming up in a hurry we had to stand and take it and such a shower is seldom seen; one continual stream of lightning all about us. Some of the men had quite a shock. After the shower we found the teem and started for camp. The first teem haveing got in just as the shower commenced. We got in at 9 o'clock wet and tired and hungry. Distance traveled today 25 miles.

June 7

Owing to the heavy rains of last night, the road was very muddy and consequently our progress was very slow this forenoon. We made about 6 miles this forenoon, together with crossing a small creek [Alcove Springs], which took nearly two hours. This afternoon we made about 15 miles, the road having dried up quite dry again. We are encamped about half a mile from the main road so as to have the benefit of a spring situated in a small ravine.

[Staples]

George got cold in the shower last night. We started late. It was quite muddy in consequence of the hard rain last night. The sun has been very hot today. We stoped two hours at noon to bait. We camped late tonight on account of not finding water to cook with. George is worse this evening.

In the interest of continuity, we continue here with David Staples' account of the tragedy that befell the Boston-Newton company.

June 8

Last night I watched with George and there was a perceptible change going on all night. I laid down this morning to sleep, was waked at 8 o'clock and we thought he was dying. He did not know us and we all gathered round him in the tent to witness the last strugle of breath leaving his body, and a most solemn sight it was. At 15 minutes past nine he ceased to breathe and God only knows the feeling in our camp and particularly his friends away from home and kindred with but 3 acceptions. As melancholy an event as was ever witnessed by man. But all and everything was done to save him but it was of no avail, and we must content ourselves with the thought that God's ways are best, yet we cannot see as he sees. Our ways are not his ways and our thoughts are not his thoughts. The company feel it hard.

Uncle Jesse [Winslow] and I serched this forenoon for a stone that could be engraved. We found a large sandstone and we engraved his name and where from and age on it in good deep large letters. His grave was dug in a conspicuous place on the main road 30 miles west of the Big Blue River in the right of the road near the junction of three tracks and a small stream runing south from it. At 5'oclock in the afternoon all being ready we assembled in the Carrale. The corps [was] brought out of the tent. Mr. Burt was requested to read scripture. He read a psalm and the last chapter of Ecleasiastees. Mr. Sweetzer made an appropriate prayer. There was not a dry eye in the group of sunburnt faces. We formed a procession and followed him to his last resting place. Each man deposited a green bough as a token of respect and the first earth was put on him at six o'clock. We returned to camp each praying the like never to happen again in our number.

Charles Gould's June 8 entry reports the sad event this way:

> Our camp was thrown into gloom and dismay by the death of Geo. Winslow.
>
> He was considered as recovering, when he caught cold by some means and relapsed worse than before. He died at 9 A.M., surrounded by his friends. This unexpected event causes us all to feel very sad.
>
> A grave was dug upon a beautiful swell of the praire. At 5 he was taken to the centre of the corral, where the funeral services were performed by reading extracts from scripture by Mr. Burt[19] and prayer by Mr. Sweetzer. He was then borne to the grave by 8 bearers and followed by the rest of the company. After his remains were lowered into the grave, all deposited a green sprig when the earth was closed upon him forever. A stone was placed at his head upon which was engraved Geo. Winslow, Newton, Ms age 25, another at his feet, marked 1849.

The president of the company, Brackett Lord, had been one of those who, along with Dr. Locke, looked after young Winslow. When the party reached Fort Kearny, he wrote a full account of the sickness, death, and burial to his wife, Clarissa Winslow Lord, who was a sister of George.

> My very beloved wife
>
> It has thus far been a pleasure for me to write to you from the fact that I have had nothing to write that you would not with pleasure peruse, but my dear wife the scene has changed and this letter will bear to you intelligence of the most unwelcome character—intelligence of the most painful for me to

---

[19] Burt wrote to his family at Newton: "No useless coffin enclosed his breast, but wrapping his sheet around him after reading Scripture and having prayer, we consigned his lifeless clay to the cold ground, beyond the reach of the howling wolves around. How little do we know what is before us! In the midst of life we are in death.'" Quoted in the Newton *Graphic*, November 27, 1896.

write and which will wring your hearts with anguish and sorrow. George is dead—what more shall I write—what can I write—but unpleasant as the news may be you will be anxious to hear the particulars.

About the 27th of May he was taken with the diareahea which lasted several days and which visibly wore upon him. He was taken the day we crossed Kansas River. He however partially recovered but on the following Tuesday he ate some pudding for dinner which hurt him and about three o'clock in the afternoon he was taken much worse, vomiting and purging, also cramping; here we stopped. He continued to grow worse & became very sick. Doct Lake [Locke], Uncle Jessee, Mr. Staples & myself watched with him during the night; about three o'clock in the morning we thought him dying. I told him of the fact, spoke to him of home, asked him if he did not wish to send some word to Eliza and his Father and mother and others—he did not leave any—seemed very sick. Wednesday morning appeared a little better and continued to improve so during the day—We remained camped during the day and untill Friday morning [George] continued to improve so much so that he wanted to start on, and the road being smooth we concluded to go on, giving him as comfortable a bed as possible in one of our large waggons, and I took charge of the wagon and drove it all the time that he rode—that he might receive all the attention that our circumstances would allow—Evening he continued about the same—Saturday we travelled part of the day, Doctor thought him improving. Sunday we moved a short distance to water and camped. Remained until Monday 10 o'clock A.M. George appeared much improved—We started on our journey. He stood the ride much better than on the previous day. We felt quite encouraged; all said that he was visibly improving. Tuesday we started at 6 o'clock A.M. George continued improving. The day was pleasant till the afternoon and George continued in good spirits. At 5 o'clock

97

P.M. there come up a most violent shower, such an one you perhaps never saw. There is nothing on these plains to break the wind and it sweeps on most furiously. The lightning is truly terrific and when accompanied with wind, hail and rain as in this case, it is truly sublime. To this storm I attribut G's death. I was however aware of its violence and guarded him as thoughroughly as possible with our rubber blankets from all dampness that might come through our covered wagons. George did not appear worse. Wednesday morning George remains the same—travelled most of the day. 3 o'clock George appeared worse. I sent immediately for the Doctor who was behind. Camped as soon as we could get to water. George did not appear better. Uncle Jessee watched the first part of the night, but George growing worse uncle Jessee called Staples and myself and we remained with him till he died. Thursday morning George was very sick and much wandering—did not know us only at intervals —seemed to fail very fast—continued to sink very fast—9 o'clock—George is *dead*—his body lays here in the tent but his spirit has fled—Our company feels deeply this solemn providence. I never attended so solemn a funeral—here we were on these plains hundreds of miles from any civilized being—and to leave one of our number was most trying. The exercises at the funeral consisted in reading the scriptures and prayer: this closed the scene—we erected grave stones on which we inscribed "George Winslow Newton Mass aged 25—1849." My dear Clarissa, you will sympathise deeply with Eliza in her affliction. What a pity that such a young family should be broken up. I hope that it may never be thus with us. George remarked several times during his sickness that he had always had a poor opinion of human nature but that he had received during his sickness more sympathy and attention than he supposed a member could receive. I am sorry that I have no particular word from him to send Eliza or his Father and Mother or you—he left none.

It was not because he did not think of home but because he thought he might get better—then at the last attack he was too sick to say anything. He used to say to me frequently, "Lord, if you are taken sick you will think more of your folks at home than yourself. I don't care anything about myself but my wife and my children they are dependent on me." I had every reason to know that he thought much of home and his folks, though he said but little. I was with him most of the time during his sickness—all the time days and most of the time nights. We did not leave him from the time he was taken sick without a watch, and here let me say that he seemed to sink away as though he was going to sleep and died without a struggle. We shall take care of all his things. It is most time for us to start and I must close this letter and leave it. I have not yet said anything to you and I cannot say much now, but I can assure you in the first place that I am well and I hope that you are all well—don't let the children forget papa. We are getting along very well and determined if possible to go through. I hope that you will not give yourself much anxiety about us in regard to sickness. I think we have passed through the most of it. All of our party are well. I must now close hoping that when I arrive in California I shall receive a letter from you. As to your getting along in my abscence, do as you think best.

Very affectionately yours,
B. Lord[20]

[20] Hansen, "A Tragedy of the Oregon Trail," pp. 124–126. In 1912 a tablet incorporating the original headstone was placed on the site by the State of Nebraska and the sons of George Winslow.

CHAPTER 7

On to Fort Laramie

The next phase of their westward venture would take the Boston-Newton company across present Nebraska to Fort Laramie, and this Plains portion of the trail was perhaps the easiest part of the journey. But, as James C. Olson has written:

> In prospect . . . that long stretch of "desert" between the Missouri and the mountains was a fearful thing to contemplate. In actuality, the emigrants learned the lessons of overland travel—the hard way—on the Plains, and this made that leg of the journey more difficult than it might have been for experienced travellers. But even had they been experienced, nothing could have alleviated the effect of the sudden and violent storms, the dust, and the oppressive monotony of travel across the Plains. Those harbingers of the mountains—Chimney Rock and Scotts Bluff—were eagerly watched for and always reached with rejoicing.[1]

We continue to present the accounts of the journey paired under the date, with Charles Gould's report appearing first.

---

[1] James C. Olson, *History of Nebraska* (Lincoln: University of Nebraska Press, 1955), pp. 65–66.

June 9

We were upon our way at 6. The morning was clear and beautiful, and the travelling excellent. The praire is not so much rolling as that which we have passed, but seems more like table land cut up with frequent gullies with short but steep banks, which in some places are difficult to descend and ascend. One company from N. York and another from Virginia, each about the same size of ours and both drawn by mules, are immediately behind us and have continued with us through the day and have encamped near us tonight. We encamped near a small, sandy ravine, which is dry with the exception of some stagnant pools. We think that we have accomplished about 25 miles today. Just before we encamped at noon, the mirage presented itself. As I was behind the train about a mile, it appeared as though the train was entering a lake of water.

[Staples]

This morning we moved on and it was with reluctance we left the grave of Brother George, but such is life. We passed today over a more level prara. We have traveled today in company with a large party from New York and Virginia. We passed today what appeared to be the bed of once a river. In this bed we found some specimans of cactus. One I noticed the center stalk had Eighty buds and blossoms. Here I killed a rattlesnake, the first I have ever seen. We camped tonight near wood and water.

Distance traveled 25 miles.

Sunday, June 10

Owing to the water being so poor, it was decided to move on as far as the Little Blue, about 6 miles distant. Accordingly, we were on our way at 5. The road was the same as yesterday, being mostly level praire or table land, with frequent and small gullies. We were all encamped again at 8 A.M. when breakfast was prepared and eaten with a keen appetite caused by the morning drive. The Little Blue is about 10 yds. wide and 8 feet deep with a rapid current. It is bordered by Oaks, Cotton Woods, Elms, &c. of good growth. Two companies passed us tonight, one from Tenn., the other from Miss. Mr. S. Nickelson of Newton[2] is in the former.

[Staples]

We started this morning before 5 o'clock and moved six miles to the banks of the Little Blue. Here we camped for the day. Brother Fred and I took a walk down the river to see if there was any game. We saw one deer and several wild turkeys. Mr. Evens [Benjamin C. Evans] was taken sick today with diarea.

June 11

There was a severe thunder shower this morning commencing at sunrise and lasting 2 hours, in consequence of which and the breaking of a wheel, we were delayed until 10½ A.M. Our route was along the bottom of the Little Blue, but owing to the rain it was quite hard travelling until the sun had dried up some of the water. The trail is quite level with exception of the frequent small gullies or ravines with steep banks, which answer as aqueducts to carry the surplus of water in the spring season. I took my rifle and followed the river bank for some miles in hopes of finding some game but was unsuccessful owing to the numerous hunters who had proceded me. We encamped at 5 with plenty of wood, water, and grass, having accomplished about 12 miles.

[Staples]

We had a hard shower this morning. Set a tire to one of our wheels and started at 11 o'clock. We have traveled today on the banks of the Blue. Plenty of wood. Nothing of note today. We camped near the party we travled with yesterday. Distance 12 miles.

---

[2] The Boston-Newton party had met Nickelson at Independence. See George Winslow's letter of May 13, p. 69. In later years Nickelson became a prominent member of the New England California Pioneer Association.

June 12

My watch came on at 1. The moon had just risen and shone forth most beautifully and no incident happening to molest me, I passed the morning very pleasantly. I aroused all hands at 4 and at 4½ we were on our way again. The road for 4 or 5 miles followed the river bottom, when it turned to the right and passed over high table land which was quite level with the exception of occasional ravines. The mirage was presented several times in distant delusive views of lake and groves of waving timber. We struck the river again at 1, when we encamped and ate our dinner with appetites that would astonish the denizens of a City. We travelled until 5 upon the river bottom when we again encamped with a plentiful supply of wood, water, and grass.

[Staples]

Today we have traveled on the bottom of the Blue. The country grows more level as we advance. This morning a fine wild turkey ran across the road and the Virginia party saw two antelopes. We camped on the Blue. Evans is quite sick tonight with diarea.

June 13

There was a tremendous thunder shower early this morning, in consequence of which we did not leave camp until late in the morning. The roads were very muddy and heavy and our progress very slow. We took our luncheon at noon of hard bread and water without taking out our team to bait.

We had the misfortune to break the pole to Mr. Evans' wagon this afternoon, but it was patched up so as to make it hold out until we reach fort Kearny if possible. We are encamped again up on the banks of the Little Blue with excellent feed for our animals, which together with our men seem quite tired out, although they have not accomplished but a very little distance today.

[Staples]

Last night we had a hard rain which makes the road bad.

Today we broke a pole in the mudhole. We camped early. Distance 12 miles.

June 14

We left our camp at half past 6 and followed along upon the banks of the Little Blue about 2 miles when we entered the table land upon the right to strike the Platte, which is said to be 20 miles distant. As we understood that there was no water in that distance, we filled up our water tanks from the delightful little creek which has supplied us so long with its refreshing water. The country which we have passed over today has been elevated table land with occasional ravines and gullies. The roads were generally pretty good, but would have been much better if the rains had been more dried up. We had the misfortune to break an axeltree today which I fear will detain us some time tomorrow.

A Deer passed within a half a mile of us today but when Staples rode after him he soon disappeared behind the hill. We encamped half past six where the grass is excellent, but neither wood or water could be obtained.

[Staples]

Today we left the Blue with regret. Passed up on a table lands.

I saw a fine deer and followed him about a mile but no use. They can see all about them on these plains. We camped off the main road ½ mile. Good grass but no wood or water. This evening we broke an axle tree to one of our best waggons in a bad crossing. Vexing to keep stoping to mend waggons. We noticed a new kind of flower today but not being a botanist could not give it a name. It was a deep orange. Distance traveled today 20 miles.

June 15

The morning is clear and beautiful but quite cold. A heavy dew has fallen thus far every night. I stayed up until 1 assisting to mend the axeltree last night and which was not

finished until 10. We started at half past ten. We soon came
in sight of the bluffs which border the Platte and travelled
until 2 before we passed through them and came upon the
bottom of the river which is about 10 miles wide. We then
stopped and lunched upon some cold fish and bread. Just
as we stopped some persons were seen at some distance which
some supposed were Indians, which caused some excitement.
Presently 2 of them came to us and we found them to be the
advance guard of a company from Washington who were
coming along the Council Bluff Road, which unites with the
other route 3 miles beyond us. They took dinner with us.
We travelled about 10 miles farther and encamped.

[Staples]

This morning was spent in putting in the axle tree. We
got started at 10 o'clock. After traveling three hours we came
in sight of the Platte River. We stoped to bait. While here
a guide to a Washington City party came up.[3] We invited
him to dine with us and gathered such information as we
could about the route. He said we were some 15 miles from
Fort Kearny, a new one haveing been built in a year or two.
We camped within 5 miles of the fort. This is in the Pawnee
Teretory.[4] We have not seen one yet. They keep off the
main road on account of the great number passing.

---

[3] The guide, whose name was Stinson, had once made a trip as far west as
South Pass. The Washington City and California Mining Association, led by
Captain Joseph Goldsborough Bruff, was organized in Washington, D.C. This
company, the Mount Washington company (organized in Boston), the
Granite State company, and the Boston-Newton company all stopped at Fort
Kearny at the same time. They remained within a day or two of travel
of one another until they reached the Great Meadows in present Nevada.

[4] The Pawnees, a confederation of Caddoan tribes, were first encountered
by white men, Coronado's party, in 1541. In historic times they inhabited the
Platte River valley of present-day Nebraska, until their removal to Indian
Territory in 1876. The Pawnees were the traditional enemy of the Sioux,
who greatly outnumbered them.

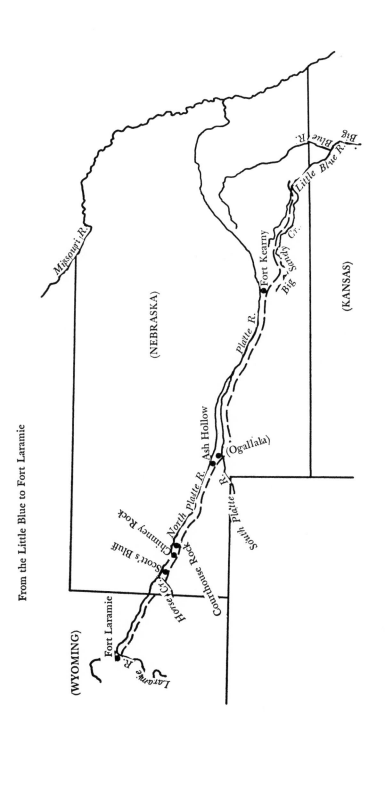

From the Little Blue to Fort Laramie

June 16

We left about 9 this morning and proceded a few miles and stopped opposite the Ft. Kearny for the rest of the day to make some repairs as has become necessary. The river bottom here is about 5 miles width and very level, being bordered upon one side with sand bluffs and the other by the river. The soil is rather sandy. Grand Island is against us and is said to be 20 miles long. There is no wood excepting upon the Island. Fort Kearny is a military station occupied by 3 companies of U.S. Troops to protect the emigrant from the Indians.[5] All the buildings are built of turf, excepting one frame house which is intended as a hospital. The situation must be very cold in the winter owing to the chance the wind has in sweeping across the Plain. There is a public house here kept by a Mormon, from whose table we once more enjoyed the luxuries of home.

[Staples]

This morning we moved up to the fort. It is made of turf with the acception of one frame house under erection. There is two companys of infantry, one of dragoons stationed here to protect emigrants and keep Indians straight. There is a boarding house here. The Officers board there and we availed ourselves of the opportunity to get a good diner once more. It was equal to any "Fremont" diner in Boston to us.

Sunday, June 17

We remained encamped today to rest our teams, &c.

We are not forgetful of this day, so sacred to all Americans, and especially to New Englanders, though however far

[5] Originally named Fort Childs, this military post was established in 1847. It was renamed in 1848 for General Stephen K. Kearny (1794–1848). Common usage added an *e* before the *y* to the name of the town which grew up there. Bruff, of the Washington City company, noted on June 17, 1849, that "this place is as yet merely the site of an intended fort; it has some adobe embankments, quarters—&c of adobe and frame, and a number of tents and sheds." See Read and Gaines, eds., *Gold Rush,* I, 22.

they may roam from home, will never forget the 17th of June.[6] I saw a Deer within a half a mile of our camp today, but he was off before my rifle could be procured. The soil near the river is quite fertile, but as you recede back towards the bluffs it grows more sandy and vegetation more scant, and the bluffs present no vegetation except a few weeds. The bluffs are mostly of sand, which the winds blow into all varieties of shape.

[Staples]

Mr. Evans is quite smart and we stop here to keep Sunday. This morning the Washington City came up and also a German company we left back. A party of five, one waggon, wants to join us. Had been traveling with the Washington company but there is two much quarreling in it to suit them. Three brothers by the name of Rohrer, one Simmons, one Morford. We have given them permission to travel a day or two to see how we like each other. This evening we had a meeting. Prayers were made by Mr. Crist and Sweetser and hymns sung. It seemed like home to hear old Hundred.[7]

The Boston-Newton company's stopover at Fort Kearny came toward the end of the wave of emigration that swept through the post in May and June of 1849. As early as mid-May more than a thousand wagons bound west had been counted.[8] In a dispatch at that time (May 18), a correspondent described the militant appearance of the travelers—every man had a gun and a revolver or two, and he mentioned that one had three Bowie knives stuck in his belt. He spoke also of a hardy fellow who had walked all the way from Maine, a long rifle on his shoulder, accompanied only by a savage-looking bulldog. More than one report stressed

[6] The anniversary of the Battle of Bunker Hill at Charleston, Massachusetts, June 17, 1745.

[7] The tune to which the Doxology is usually sung.

[8] Information in this paragraph and the following paragraph from *Publications of the Nebraska State Historical Society*, XX (1922), 194–206.

that the great problem of the emigrants was too much baggage. Thousands of pounds of flour and bacon were offered for sale at a dollar a hundred, and if there were no takers the provisions were abandoned by the trail. Flannel shirts were selling for a dime, wagons at five to twenty-five dollars, "and everything else in proportion."

To give some idea of the volume of traffic: on May 21, 214 wagons passed the fort, making 1,203 to that date, not counting a military train of 50 wagons. On May 28, 460 rolled by; on May 29, 381; on May 31, 194; and on June 2, 470 were reported in the last two days. By sundown of June 9, according to the correspondent who signed himself "Pawnee," the number had mounted to 5,092, exclusive of 250 government wagons. From then on the traffic began to taper off. On June 23, five days after the Boston-Newton party moved on, the correspondent wrote: "The great California caravan has at length swept past this point, and the prairies are beginning to resume their wonted state of quietness and loneliness. Occasionally a solitary wagon hurries on . . . ." The grand total of wagons reported by this date was 5,516 on the south bank of the river and about 600 on the other side. It was estimated that there were 20,000 men on the road between Fort Kearny and Fort Hall.

On June 18 the Boston-Newton company left Fort Kearny, as Charles Gould recorded.

June 18

We were delayed until 11 in repairing a wheel which has caused us more trouble and vexation than it is worth. Our road was very hard, dry and perfectly level and consequently we made a good distance although our day was short. We camped a little after 5 with most excellent grass for our cattle. We obtained water by digging a hole 4 feet deep, which was filled with quite decent water in the morning. A company of 5 persons from Mo. and 1 wagon have joined in with our train.

[Staples]

We left the fort and passed up on the river bottom. Saw several antelope and a most beautiful flower—a deep red— the root of which when cooked tastes like potatoes and makes a good pickle.[9] We camped off the river and to get water we had to dig a well. We got good water by diging three feet. Distance traveled 15 miles.

June 19

We started at 6 with a beautiful morning and clear air. Our road followed the river bottom as yesterday, sometimes coming within a mile of the river, and at other times diverging several miles. The road has been level, dry and smooth. The winds have blown with great force today, driving the dry dust and sand around, penetrating every crack and crevice about the wagons and causing us great trouble by having sore eyes. We encamped tonight near the banks of a small creek that empties into the Platte at this point. The grass is quite good, and the water, though not very good, was very plenty.

[Staples]

We made a good drive. Nothing of note. Made 25 miles.

Although they are clearly reporting the same events, Gould and Staples assign some of the happenings to different days in the following three entries. The dating again synchronizes starting with June 23.

June 20

There was a very heavy thunder storm in the night which came with such violence as almost to upset our wagons.

---

[9] Edwin Bryant called this root the prairie potato. Wild peas also grew in this area and were used by the emigrants, as were herbs and various other plants—dandelions, plantain, clover, mustard, sorrel, etc.—which were cooked as greens. See Bradford Augier, *Free for the Eating* (Harrisburg, Pennsylvania: Stackpole Books, 1966), pp. 70–152, esp. 132.

We got started at 5½. The travelling was very hard owing to the rain which fell last night. The company from Virginia followed immediately after us, but the N.Y. company stopped to recruit. I took my rifle and went over to the bluffs to explore them. Before I reached them I came across a praire dog village. These curious little animals would sit at the mouth of their holes and bark until you approached within 6 or 8 rods, when they would jump into their holes and others would stick out their heads and bark.

We encamped at 4 in consequence of a thunder shower which burst upon us with terrible fury and violence just as we got our animals picketed.

[Staples]

Today has been hot. We have had to lay by at noon three hours. We have to eat hard bread and make our coffee with Buffalo chips for the first time. We look now anxious for Buffallo. Distance 20 miles.

June 21

The roads are muddy and heavy again today and the train moves very slow and hard. We did not get under way until 7 this morning. Our road lead along the river bank, sometimes being quite wet and marshy, at other times more dry, the scenery presented being the same as we have passed through thus far on the Platte. The sand bluffs represented miniature mountain scenery to perfection, the winds and rains having worked them out into all varieties of form and shape.

After you have entered them, you find yourselves lost in the ravines and winding, sometimes being oblidged to retrace your step to get clear of them. The Doctor went upon a Buffalo hunt across the river in company with 2 of the Rohrer company. They found 2 or 3 and gave chase to them, but did not succeed in stopping them. Several Antelopes have been seen but they always keep beyond rifle shot.

[Staples]

We have made good time today and camped near wood and water. We have seen quite a number of Cactus beds blossom pale yellow.

Distance 20 miles.

June 22

The morning is pleasant and we are off in good season. We made our first attempt in burning Buffalo Chips last night, but owing to their being wet yesterday, they did not burn very free. Mr. Coffey and myself slept upon the ground last night. The travelling is very hard this forenoon, but it has been better this afternoon. We think that we have travelled about 20 miles today.

We found a spring of cold water shaded by Oaks, which was a luxury duly appreciated by us. We encamped about 1 mile beyond the spring.

The mosquitoes have been terribly thick this night, troubling the cattle so much that they could feed but a very little, many of them running and pulling up their pickets. The road here recedes from the river and runs nearly under the bluffs.

[Staples]

The river bottom narrows and the Bluffs grow higher. Today noon we saw distinctly on the opposite side of the river two Buffallo.

Two of Rohrer's party and the Dr of our party went after them. Returned. Had a chase but did not get one. We camped late without wood or water except what we brought from the river a mile. Distance 23 miles.

June 23

The animals have been worried so much by the mosquitoes that they are in poor condition to travel. They have swarmed about them all night keeping them in a continuous chafe. Many of our men have not been able to sleep also in consequence of them. The road approaches still nearer the bluffs, in some instances passing over them, but the bluffs are not near as high as they have been, being more like rolling praire. The trail has been very hard and dry. Just after we had encamped at noon, several buffalo were seen on the plain about 2 miles distant. This caused great excitement amongst our men, many of whom left their dinners and started in pursuit of them. The Buffaloes instantly started for the bluffs, where our men pursued them, but their chase proved fruitless as they did not again get sight of them. Some hunters from the Virginia company having captured 2, they gave us what we wanted from one of them. The meat was excellent and proved quite a luxury.

[Staples]

We are now in the Sioux country[10] and this afternoon one of the Virginia party shot a large Buffalo. They gave us as much as we wanted. A party of our men went out from out camp but did not get one.

We camped near a running brook for Sunday. Distance traveled 20 miles.

Sunday, June 24

I was aroused quite early this morning by the cry of Buffaloes, and upon the bottom at a distance of a mile several were seen feeding. Looking up to the bluffs—many of them being quite covered with them—several of our men instantly got their breakfast and started immediately to hunt them amongst them myself. After going 4 or 5 miles, we found ourselves in the midst of them. Every hill top was covered with them. I crawled up to a herd who were drinking in a

---

[10] The Teton, or western, comprised the largest division of the Sioux, and included the Oglala, Brulé, Blackfoot (not to be confused with the Algonquian-speaking Blackfoot tribe), Sans Arc, Miniconjou, Two Kettle, and Hunkpapa bands. First encountered by Father Hennepin in 1680 on the Upper Mississippi, they migrated westward, and by 1800 were located on the Upper Missouri.

pool of water. Some were rolling in the dirt and others stood quietly around. There were some huge old Bulls, and some Cows, Heifers and Calves. As I lay watching them, another person came up on the opposite bluff and frightened all away except 5 old Bulls. Although I was some distance from them, I fired at one. He instantly started and ran a few feet, when he turned around and faced me a few seconds and then started over the hills.

[Staples]

This morning before sunrise the cry of Buffalo was raised and every man was out to see one of those animals we had long looked for. Within a mile of our camp were fifteen large ones feeding, and back on the Bluffs a mile or two there were hundreds on every hill top. It was two strong a temptation for us who had never seen any game larger than a partridge. Several of us took our rifles and went out to get a nearer view of the "elephant."[11] We had gone a couple of miles and came direct on a large hurd. We layed behind a rise of ground some 30 rods from them. We watched them some time and we were getting ready to shoot when they discovered us and off they started on a kind of clumsy gate [gait]. I had the sattisfaction of putting a ball in one of those Old Bulls just back of the foreshoulder. He hobled off, evidently feeling the worse for the opperation.

There was one seen in the direction he went off some hour after streched out for good. They will go a good ways with a half ounce ball in them unless it passes through their lounges. To prove this Mr. Nichols, Esterbrook, and I could not give it up, so, we started for another drove some mile and half off. We crept up to them as near as ten rods and all three of us put a ball in an old bull. He made off. Ran more than a half mile before he showed signes of haveing

---

[11] In popular speech at this time, the word *elephant* connoted the unbelievable.

been hit. We followed him and had the sattisfaction of seeing him lay down. We got near enough and let him have three more balls and he never tried to rise but yealded up the ghost. This was my first attempt at Buffalo hunting. We skined up a place, took out a few pounds of the best stake, and returned to camp at noon. We went after them on foot and was tired traveling over these sand bluffs. On coming to camp it was all excitement and we soon had a party of ten to go out and bring in the Meat. We found a hurd near by the one we shot and could not deny ourselves the pleasure of one charge. We started and our horses entered into the spirit of the chase and we were soon along side of a mighty herd—full five hundred darting over the prara at full speed. Such feelings of delight I never realized before. Brother Fred had the pleasure of one charge mounted on an Indian poney. On fireing the horses turned as though they were trained to the chase. After loading four mules with the best of the meat we left well satisfied with our first attempt.[12]

June 25

Our road followed over the bluffs about 10 miles when we struck directly across the bottom to strike the river. Our road was very good until we reached the river bottom, when it became soft and muddy. We crossed the lower ford, the road continuing on further up the river to the upper ford. The river is about 3/4 of a mile wide here. The bottom is quicksand, which makes it very difficult for the mules to travel. The water is from 1 to 3 feet deep. We were obliged to take half the load from our wagon in order to enable the mules to draw them across and then it proved very difficult. It took until late at night to get all our things across. This

[12] The buffalo hunt took place near present Ogallala, Nebraska. Dr. Dean Jewett Locke also brought down a buffalo, and in later years often told his sons about the experience, proudly displaying the buffalo robe made from the hide.

is the South Fork, we having passed the Division with[out] knowing it. We encamped upon the north bank.

[Staples]

This morning we were moveing in season. Mules well rested. We came to the crossing of the South Fork of the Platte River at eliven o'clock. We baited an hour and commenced to cross. The stream here is full a mile wide. This crossing is a new one and 20 miles below where Bryant crossed.[13] The afternoon was spent in getting our teems over, haveing to lighten considerable and packed it over on horses and mules. The quicksand and deep places rendered it almost impossible for the teem to draw. We camped on the opposite side of the river without wood and verry few chips. This evening the Verginia company are crossing a government waggon is on the opposite side. Dis. 10 m.

June 26

Owing to some of our men being obliged to cross the river to get some luggage which had been left over there, we did not get under way until 9. Our road for a few miles followed up the north bank of the south fork, when it started directly over the bluffs to the North Fork about 3 miles distant. The bluffs were quite high and the view from the tops was very beautiful. The bluffs upon the south of the South Fork as far as the eye could reach were covered with Buffaloes. We travelled for a few miles upon the south bank of the North Fork and encamped with a plentiful supply of grass. Mosquitoes were very plenty.

[Staples]

This forenoon we passed up the left bank of the South Fork. Soon after noon halt we struck the bluffs. To cross over to the north fork at the place we crossed to it the two

[13] Bryant's crossing is described in his *What I Saw in California: Being the Journal of a Tour . . . Across the Continent . . . in the Years 1846, 1847* (5th ed.; New York, 1849), p. 94.

rivers were not more than three miles apart but verry high hills between. We camped tonight near the river without wood but with plenty of musquitoes.

June 27

We got away at 6 this morning. Our route for a few miles followed the river bottom, when the bluffs came so near the river that we were obliged to strike into the bluffs. There was considerable rise, but after we had reached the heights it was quite level. It was mostly a plain hollowed out like a basin. We continued along the tops of the bluffs until nearly night, when we entered a ravine of very curious and romantic scenery and passed into the river bottom again. We observed a shower rising, which we supposed at a considerable distance from us, but when we entered the bottom from the ravine it was almost upon us and it burst upon us in a few minutes. We passed on about a mile and encamped.

[Staples]

Today the road has been some sandy. Not anything of note till just as night [fell] several of us started off for some wood a mile distant. It proved to be a few willows, the worst of wood to burn. We found a spring of cold water three feet deep and such things are a rarity in these parts. We drank harty. Tonight we camp near the river and of all imaginable pests the musquitoes excede all at this place. This is the hardest camp we have had to sleep. We expect to be troubled the rest of the way on this river. We have noticed some new kinds of cactus. The most abundant kind is of a pale yellow blossom and they grow in large beds, as many as a hundred buds and blossoms on one root. Distance traveled today 20 miles.

June 28

We followed along the river bottom until the middle of the afternoon when the trail turns suddenly to the left over a very steep bluff which was very difficult for the teams to ascend. It then followed amongst the hills and ravines through scenery of the most variable beauty that ever I saw. After going in this manner 1 mile when we struck into a deep ravine, called Ash Hollow,[14] which led into the bottom again. The road which comes from the upper ford passes through this ravine. We here found some beautiful springs of water and also some ash trees which line the ravine. We found the Virginia company encamped here and Mr. Crist, who was partaking of some supper with them, was accidentally shot by a member of their company with a revolver. The Doctors have examined him but cannot determine the extent of the wound. We encamped half a mile from Ash Hollow.

[Staples]

Today has been rather hard drive. We have passssed over a good deal of hardy sandy Bluffs. Today we have found wood and three of the finest springs man ever quenched his thirst at. This afternoon we had one of the hardest pulls we have ever had to get on a rise before going into Ash Hollow. This is a most beautifull place. We found the Verginia party camped in the mouth of the Hollow. Mr. Crist, the gentleman that joined us at Independence, went to see them. They asked him to take some supper. He sat eating and one of the party had a revolver and by accident it went off. The ball passing through his arm struck a rib and passed around saving his life, whereas if it had struck between his ribs it would have killed him. We camped near by. Distance traveled 23 miles.

June 29

We remain encamped today in consequence of Mr. Crist's accident. The Physicians have made another examination

[14] On September 3, 1855, Ash Hollow was the scene of General W. S. Harney's massacre of a band of Brulé Sioux. Wild flowers still grow there, among them the pentstemon. One of these flowers lies between the pages of Gould's diary.

this morning and have found the ball to have been lodged near his backbone, having passed through his arm and then struck his rib and thence passed around to his back. They consider his wound as not being fatal, and think that he will be able to travel tomorrow. We are improving this opportunity to repair a wheel which had got out of order, whilst our animals were also resting and recruiting. As there is a plentiful supply of wood, the cooks are improving the opportunity of baking a supply of bread.[15]

Just before sundown an Indian village came up the river and encamped opposite to us. They had a great many horses and mules. We supposed the village to number 150 men, women and children.

[Staples]

Today we lay by on Mr. Crist's account. He is better and we hope to move tomorrow. Our cooks have been busy baking here. Plenty of wood and good spring water. We have now filled a wheel today and rearranged our loads. All well in camp now but the shot man.

June 30

Mr. Crist was placed in a wagon upon an air bed where he rode quite comfortably. Our route lay along the river as usual. The trail was very sandy, causing our progress to be very slow and tedious for the team. It is not supposed that we have made more than 12 miles today. The bluffs have assumed a very picturesque and fanciful appearance. They are composed mostly of soft stone which is worked by the winds and waters into the various forms in which we behold them. The mosquitoes are very troublesome, it being almost impossible to drive them away.

[15] Just how bread was baked on the trail remains a mystery to me. George Thomason may have used Conant's Patent Yeast, a product advertised in the Boston newspapers prior to the company's departure.

The grass has been quite scarce today and but for the plentiful rains of this season, there would probably have been none.

[Staples]

This morning we were moveing early, fixing Mr. Christ a bed in the waggon. We passed on over a sandy hard road, the Bluffs coming down to the river. The country grows more sterile and the grass. We camped at 5 o'clock. Distance traveled 15 miles. Just at night a white wolf passed ahead of the train. I took a rifle and after following him a short distance put a ball in his hip, which stoped his progress. Our dog had a clinch with him. His teeth were like sheers when they came together. This is the first one we could get near enough to shoot at.

Sunday, July 1

Our horses and mules were taken up and harnessed at the sound of the bugle which one of the Rohrer company have with them.[16] The road has become hard and dry with only sand spots at great distances from one another. The bluffs on this side of the river are much more level than they have been, while on the opposite, bluffs are much more abrupt.

It has been exceedingly warm today, which, together with the dust and mosquitoes, makes it very unpleasant travelling. We encamped at 6 by the side of a small creek of decent water. We suppose that we have made about 25 miles today.

We have made fires of buffalo chips all around the Corral to drive the mosquitoes away from the animals.

[Staples]

We have commenced this month by a fine drive. We camped on a fine creek of clear water and good grass. Nothing of note. We passed a large company who were laid by for Sunday. Distance traveled 25 miles.

[16] Because of the June 29 stopover necessitated by the injury to Crist, the company evidently voted to make up the lost day by traveling on Sunday.

July 2

The morning was rather cloudy. After a few miles we came in sight of the *Chimney Rock,* a remarkable landmark at a probable distance of 15 miles. About 12 miles on this side of that was another bluff worn out by the winds and rains so as to represent from some views the form of a building. It is called the *Court House,* one view giving it the appearance of a large building with wings, surmounted by a dome, other views giving it the appearance of a building in decay. It is very large, being several hundred feet in height and length. It is composed of a very soft stone or hardened sand. It is situated about 5 miles from the trail on the left. The travelling has been excellent and we have made about 25 miles. We are encamped about 5 miles from the Chimney Rock.

[Staples]

We got an early start this morning. Made our noon halt opposite Court House bluff. After noon several of our party went over to take a look at it. I climed to the top and engraved my name, and such a view man seldom sees. We overtook the train just before camping. Camped tonight on a Bluff two miles from the river, no wood or water. Distance traveled 25 miles.

July 3

5 miles brought us to the *Chimney Rock,* which is situated about 1 mile to the left of the trail. This remarkable curiosity is what remains of a sand bluff which has been worked by the wind and water into the shape which we now behold it. It is said to be 250 feet high and formerly was twice that height, but it is fast crumbling away. It can be seen on a clear day at a distance of 40 miles.

A little farther other bluffs are shaped into fanciful forms representing various kinds of decayed and ancient ruins. The trail has been excellent. Scotts Bluffs have been

121

in sight all of the afternoon. Just before reaching them, the trail leaves the river and runs in the rear of them. We encamped within 1 mile of them and the view is beautiful.

[Staples]

Last night two men that formerly belonged to the Dayton, Ohio, company came to camp and wanted to stop the night with us. Their party has broken—some gone back. These were returning hartily sick of the trip. This morning we were of[f] in good season. We camped some 5 miles before reaching Chimney Rock. This we thought worthy of a visit, it being one mile of[f] the main road. Before reaching it we passed several new-made graves. We found a spring near the rock coming out of a clay bluff, cold and reviving. We climed up the base of Chimney Rock some two hundred feet, engraved our names and returned to the party. They halted at noon near the river, five miles beyond the rock. Good grass. This afternoon we left the river near Scott *Bluff*.[17] Here we *filled* our water tanks. We traveled near the Bluffs some four miles from the river. Distance traveled 25 miles.

July 4

We are all mindful of this day—the pride of all Americans.

The cooks have prepared some doughnuts (a great rarity) which, together with some cheese which had been preserved for the occasion, gave us a treat not to be despised. After they were distributed, Mr. Felch proposed 3 cheers for the birthday of our country, which was heartily responded to. Mr. F. then proposed 3 more for our friends at home whose hearts swell with love for us and whose best wishes are for

---

[17] A national monument since 1919, Scotts Bluff was the first butte of dominating height seen by travelers on the Oregon Trail. The name commemorates a tragic episode of fur-trading days: Hiram Scott, an American Fur Company trader, fell ill and was deserted by his companions. His skeleton was found at the foot of the bluff by a party the next year.

CHARLES GOULD
This painting, which dates from 1844,
shows Gould in his twentieth year.

DAVID STAPLES
Staples is shown here as he appeared in
1860, at the age of thirty-six.

The monument at the site of George Winslow's grave on the Oregon Trail near Fairbury, Nebraska, incorporates the original marker. The monument was dedicated on October 12, 1912.

BRACKETT LORD
This photograph of the president of the Boston-Newton company was taken about 1860.

GEORGE WINSLOW
This likeness of George Winslow was made in 1849, shortly before the company's departure from Boston.

A monument at Shingle Springs, California, marks the site on which the Boston-Newton party camped on September 26, 1849—their last campsite on the trail. The inscription on the monument, which was erected in June, 1950, was composed by the author.

our welfare. This was responded to with great feeling by all present.

We passed in the rear of Scotts Bluffs through a beautiful and level valley bordered on both sides by fanciful bluffs. We passed from the valley over a high ridge, from the top of which we had our first view of the Rocky Mountains. We found a spring of water cold as ice just as we were leaving the valley. We are encamped on *Horse Creek*, 12 miles from the ridge.

[Staples]

This is the nation's birthday and as Americans our liveliest thoughts are called out in gratitude for the day that declared us an independant people. We could not celebrate it much in the usual way, but our thoughts were at home and we made the hills ring with our cheers for the day and fond ones at home. Small arms were used to make a noise. We halted at noon near a verry cold spring just before crossing the Bluffs. Here we found there was a log house up [belonging to] a Blacksmith who kept a store.[18] He bought his goods of Emigrants who find they have to[o] much, and most of them do. We sold him a bag of coffee. Pork he would not take as a gift. Has made a good deal of money by mending wagons &c. He has a Squaw of the Sioux tribe for a wife. Here we passed two large companys who were repairing. Just after leaveing this trading post we came up on a Bluff and we beheld for the first time the Rocky Mountains. One prominent peak[19] arose far above the surrounding hills and was a majestick sight. We had longed to see it for some weeks. We camped tonight near a creek of fine water and good grass. Distance 20 m.

---

[18] Probably Antoine Robidoux, a brother of Joseph Robidoux who founded the city of St. Joseph.

[19] Laramie Peak.

July 5

Our road has led over very barren sand hills for several miles, which made it very hard travelling. We then struck for river bottom again, where the road was excellent. We nooned by the side of a small stream that follows along the side of the Platte which was very cool and clear, resembling our New England streams. Several of our men took the seine and catched 70 small but excellent fish from this beautiful little stream. The country presents a more barren aspect as we advance toward the mountains.

We are encamped where the forage is miserable, what little grass there was having dried up.

[Staples]

We were off in season this morning. This country grows more sterile and on the left bank of the river nothing but sand hills were seen. We were most fortunate in coming up to a capital spring in time for dinner. It is the largest we had seen, furnishing quite a stream and tributary to the river. Good grass on the banks of the creek. After dinner our boys took the sein and caught seventy fine fish out of the clear spring water. They were nice and hard. I am surprised that Bryant did not discover it. We have made a long drive today. Camped at half past Eight. Poor grass. The grass seems much more parched up here than it has been back. Distance traveled today 30 miles. Good.

July 6

Six miles brought us to the forks of the Platte and Learimie. We forded Learimie River at $\frac{1}{4}$ of a mile from the fork and 1 mile below Ft. Learimie. The stream is quite clear and has a swift current. We nooned on the opposite shore and then moved out about 4 miles to the bank of the Platte and encamped. The soil is very barren and sandy and has a most desolate appearance. Ft. Learimie was built by the N. W. Fur Co. and occupied by them until this season when it was purchased by government as a military station.[20] I have not had time to visit it.

[Staples]

We acerttained by a party returning that we were near the fort. We started early, came up to the crossing at 10 o'clock. There were several parties crossing. After waiting an hour we had our turn. This crossing was on the Larime near the junction of the *Platte.* The water ran very rapid and was near three feet deep. We got all safely over without wetting our load much. We crossed opposite Ft. John[21] one mile below Ft. *Larima.* These places are nothing but a mud wall with quarters for a company of a hundred men. The government have lately bought it of the A. Fur Com [American Fur Company] and are getting ready to create a new one near by. Here we saw some hundred or two waggons deserted to pack, and pork was piled up all about. We found that we had Eight hundred [lbs.] more of the swine than we

---

[20] Originally a fur-trading post, Fort William was built by William Sublette (for whom it was named) and Robert Campbell in June, 1834, and sold to the American Fur Company in 1835. The company sold it to the government in 1849, and it became a military post on June 26 of that year. When a new adobe fort was built to replace Fort William, it "was christened Fort John, presumably in honor of John B. Sarpy, an officer of the company that built and owned it. But this name did not 'take.' Instead, the name Laramie, given to the river and region and frequently applied to the preceding wooden fort, soon attached itself to the new adobe structure." Leroy R. Hafen and F. M. Young, *Fort Laramie and the Pageant of the West, 1843–1890* (Glendale, Calif.: Arthur H. Clark Co., 1938), p. 70. Bryant refers to "Fort Laramie, or 'Fort John,' as it is otherwise called" in *What I Saw in California,* p. 109.

[21] Apparently this is a reference to Fort Platte, as Fort John was one of the names of Fort Laramie (see note 20, above). "Fort Platte was a commodious adobe structure located on the right bank of the North Platte, about three-quarters of a mile above the mouth of the Laramie. Its erection [in 1839] doubtless stimulated the building of Fort William in more substantial form." Hafen and Young, *Fort Laramie and the Pageant of the West, 1834–1890,* p. 69.

should actually need. We sold it for ¾ cents pr pound. We moved three miles from the crossing up the river and camped near a spring, calculating to stop tomorrow to rest our mules and repair our waggons. There has not been any rain here for 35 days and the roads are verry dry. The wheels are shrinking. Tires get loose. Distance traveled 8 miles.

CHAPTER 8

Fort Laramie to South Pass

The newly commissioned military post of Fort Laramie, where the Boston-Newton company stopped for rest and repairs, was an adobe structure whose walls enclosed about three-quarters of an acre of ground. There were watchtowers on the walls; and when Edwin Bryant saw it, two cannons—brass swivels—defended the gate. "On three sides of the court, next to the walls, are various offices, store rooms, and mechanical shops. The other side is occupied by the main building of the fort, two stories in height."[1]

One forty-niner, Alonzo Delano, wrote that

> Its neat, white-washed walls presented a welcome sight to us, after being so long from anything like a civilized building, and the motley crowd of emigrants, with their array of wagons, cattle, horses, and mules gave a pleasant appearance of life and animation.[2]

The stretch of country that lay between Fort Laramie and the Continental Divide would put the Boston-Newton company to a severe test. At the fort the elevation was 4,230 feet; one

---

[1] Bryant, *What I Saw in California*, p. 109, cited in Harold F. Taggart, ed., "The Journal of David Staples," p. 148.

[2] Alonzo Delano, *Life on the Plains and Among the Diggings* (Auburn, N.Y., 1854), p. 76.

127

hundred miles beyond, it rose to 5,123 feet, increasing to 7,550 feet at the summit of South Pass. Not only was the trail difficult, but forage was poor and the travelers were under the constant necessity to lighten their loads. According to a report written on August 19, 1849, at Green River in present Wyoming:

> From Laramie grass began to fail our stock, and the utmost diligence had to be used to sustain them. From thence after the first fifty miles, dead cattle and fragments of wagons came in sight, and as far as here, I have counted about one thousand wagons that have been burnt or otherwise disposed of on the road. Destruction seems to have been the prevailing emotion of everybody who had to leave anything on the trip. Wagons have been wantonly sacrificed without occasion by hundred, being fired for the apparent purpose of preventing them from being serviceable to anybody else. . . .
>
> From Deer creek to the summit, the greatest amount of property has been thrown away. Along the banks of the Platte to where the Sweetwater road turns off, the amount of valuable property thrown away is astonishing—iron, trunks, clothing, etc., lying strewed around to the value of fifty thousand dollars in about twenty miles. I have counted about five hundred dead oxen along the road, and only *three* mules. . . .[3]

This leg of the journey would take the Boston-Newton company to what David Staples rightly called the turning point— South Pass, the gateway through the Rocky Mountains, discovered in 1824 by Thomas Fitzpatrick, a trader for the American Fur Company.[4] The pass marked the halfway point in the two-

[3] "Joaquin," in the *Daily Missouri Republican*, October 25, 1849, reprinted in *Publications of the Nebraska State Historical Society*, XX (1922), 212–213.

[4] Although Robert Stuart and his party of returning Astorians crossed through South Pass on October 22, 1812, it is probable that they were unaware of their discovery. Fitzpatrick's discovery was publicized by General William H. Ashley, head of the American Fur Company.

thousand-mile journey from Independence to the mines of California.

In this chapter, as previously, Gould's account is presented first in the day-by-day narration.

July 7

We are stopped today to rest our animals and repair our wagons and also to arrange our loads and to make all possible reduction in them. It was voted that no member should carry more than 100 lbs. unless he paid 25 cts. per pound for all extra.

[Staples]

This day has been spent in overhauling loads and repairing waggons, and the members limited to one hundred pounds including arms, ammunition &c. We find we can lighten considerable in chains, barrels, and everything is ready for an early start tomorrow. We found a mile from camp a man left by some party. He was deranged and sick with a verry bad diarea. Our Dr gave him some medicine and something to eat, but could not get him to camp. He is entirely naked and sunburnt. A pitiable object. We shall take some measures to get him to the Fort. The party that left him are verry censurable, hardly human. This evening it looks like rain. Hope to have a shower. Our camp is pleasantly set out with cactus—the pineapple and a new species to me, having a verry fine red flower. Today our boys picked quite a mess of wild currents and for sauce they are a treat.

Sunday, July 8

We followed the river bottom for several miles when it suddenly enters the Black Hills through a deep gorge of perpendicular walls. The trail here turns to the left and passes over the hills which were quite steep and rough. We nooned upon the top of one of them and were so fortunate as to find the feed pretty good. We kept upon the hills the

129

rest of the day and encamped where the grass was very good, which was quite pleasing to us as the feed was mostly very miserable upon the road. At our last encampment on the Platte, we found a man who was insane. We could gather nothing satisfactory of him as to who he was or where he came from. His clothing consisted of a shirt and pants, both badly torn. He had a fire over which he performed many strange maneuvers. He also had some provisions which some of the emigrants had left for him.

[Staples]

We camped yesterday three miles from the fort on the Platte. We got our tire reset and this morning we were off in season. I went over to carry letters to the Fort. Our party kept up the river road. I struck across the Bluffs by "Warm Spring" laid down by Bryant. The upper one was as clear a spring as was ever seen, discharging a large quantity of water. I came up with the company at two o'clock, haveing taken the wrong road four miles. We now begin to find it uphill work as we near the Mounts. We passed a creek that had the appearance of lately having been swollen.

Moveing some of the bushes and driftwood we found large quantities of *hail*, the stones after a warm day as large as pees. We camped tonight on a rise some 20 miles from the *fort*. Fair grass. The road has not run as formerly near the river. It keeps us today on the bluffs more, occasionaly comeing in sight of the river. We have passed one party with *Oxen*. Distance traveled 22 m.

July 9

We were on our way in good season this morning. The road was very hard and smooth through hills for some distance, when it lead to the Platte bottom again. We nooned at Horse Shoe Creek where the water and grass was excellent. We made a long halt to enable our animals to get thoroughly filled, as it is extremely doubtful when we shall get any more good feed. The trail followed along the river bottom and was very smooth and level. We travelled until 8½ tonight and encamped where the feed was tolerable upon the banks of the Platte. The river frequently passes through deep cuts of rock 2 or 300 ft. in height, the sides of which are perpendicular. The stone in some places is about the color of brick, which it resembles very much at a distance.

[Staples]

This morning we were off in season at 9 o'clock. We came to [a] cold clear spring. These springs are soule-reviveing as we came uppon them unexpected. Five miles from this spring we came to fine creek water, clear and cold. Abundance of grass, timber &c. This was the best nooning place we have had. Here we found a party throwing away their bacon to lighten their loads. We met several return[ing] trains, all ox teams. Report poor grass ahead. We traveled late and camped on the Platte a few miles above where the river makes through the ridge called by Frémont the *Cannon*. Good grass. Today we passed several parties of ox teams. Now we have the advantage of oxen. Distance 25.

July 10

The road again leaves the river and passes over the hills in a nearly southerly direction for 12 or 15 miles. The road was very hilly, the road ascending all of the way nearly and was very hard and smooth. The forage is miserable and the prospect looks rather discouraging for our animals. We were so fortunate as to [find] a supply for our animals' dinner in a small ravine through which the water runs in the spring. We have found some fine springs. We have reset 3 of our wheel tires, which the dry atmosphere has rendered necessary. The trail is still ascending until about night, when it takes a westerly course and descends very fast into the valley through which run a small road and stream. The prospect from the high hills was the most beautiful and romantic that

131

I ever beheld. We could not find any grass at all for our animals and we were obliged to *corral* them without any supper.

[Staples]

Today we have had a verry uneaven road working around Laramie. At noon hour we had to run of[f] the road some half mile [at the] side of a small creek. Wood, water, and grass. Here we reset several of our tire[s]. The sun is hot and air verry drying. The woodwork to our waggons shrink verry much. We moved at four o'clock. We camped tonight on the banks of a small stream. Not a spear of grass. This is the first time our teems have had to be tied up without some feede. The guidebook says some 17 miles we find a stream, grass, and water. We have found several glorious good springs, the water boiling up out of the clear sand. We found camped here severall parties that passed us some time since while [we were] laying by with our sick. We have several unwell from diarea &c. Distance traveled today 20 miles.

July 11

My watch came on the last half of the night. The moon shone clear and beautiful. Everything was hushed in silence excepting the occasional braying of the mules, who were obliged to go without anything to eat. We were on our way again at sunrise in hopes that we would soon fall in with some feed for our mules and stopped at 7 where there was a pitiful allowance of grass and baited until 9. The country is very hilly and the soil very poor and dry. It was composed of red sandstone and clay for several miles. We nooned at a very small allowance of grass the mules picked out from among the wild sage brush, which almost cover the ground. The road has been hard and smooth but hilly this afternoon. We are again under the necessity of encamping without feed, which casts a gloom over the members which cannot be concealed.

[Staples]

This morning we moved early out five miles. Found some grass and turned out two hours here. Our mules got quite refreshed. We have passed over a verry hilly country. This afternoon we could not find a green patch of grass and were obliged to bait on dried up Buffalo grass. We camped on a small stream now, but has the appearance of quite a river in a wet time. We could not find near this stream grass enough for one mule. We tied our teems up with a view of an early start. Distance traveled 25 miles.

July 12

I worked in company with some of the members until 12½ o'clock last night in repairing the wheels which had become shrunk by the very dry atmosphere of this climate. The trail is again hard and dry, passing over hills and through valleys. There is no grass, the drought having dried up everything green. We stopped at noon upon the banks of a beautiful little stream the name of which I could not learn. By driving our mules down the stream half a mile, they found quite tolerable picking, which seemed to revive them. We arrived at Deer Creek at 5 P.M. near its junction with the Platte. There were several hundred encamped here, but the grass was all fed for some distance, the animals being driven several miles up the creek. We encamped here where the grass was green but fed very close. The sound of the blacksmith's hammer was heard in every direction which, together with the music and busy hum of voices, seemed like a settled village.[5]

---

[5] J. Goldsborough Bruff, captain of the Washington City company, which arrived at this campsite on July 16, spoke of "passing through hundreds of tents, wagons, camp fires, and people of every age & sex, congregated on the banks of Deer Creek. . . . The abandonment of property here—at Deer Creek, is extraordinary." He mentioned seeing "A Diving Bell and all the apparatus, heavy anvils, iron and steel, forges, bellows, lead . . . bacon in

[Staples]

Today we have made a good drive to arrive at Deer Creek. We passed several streams but the banks are grazed as close as sheep can perform that duty. This forenoon we saw a buffallo. I followed a short distance, the ground so uneven my horse could not keep up with him. We baited at noon near a cold spring. These springs coming out of the hills are a perfect "God send" to the traveler. The road has been over hills and bluffs. We struck the Platte some five miles before arriveing at Deer Creek. A mile further we saw at a distance a buffalo. Mr. Whittier and I started after him. It proved to be one that had been shot. Today we saw several carcases indicating that they were here. We took a survey and to our joy we [saw] three at a distance. We made for them. By hideing behind the hills we came directly upon them. I put a ball in back of the foreshoulder. He went on. I loded up and started my horse slowly and succeeded in comeing up to him and putting a ball in his back. It is difficult to shoot on the full gallop. We though[t] we had him. He laging behind the others, we came up to him. I headed him and he stoped. I fired at his head. He droped on his knees and came up and with a tremendous rush came directly at me. My horse was to[o] quick for him and saved me a shock.

We followed him slowly, expecting to see him fall. He was bleeding freely and his lungs was evidently pierced as the Blood was running of[f] his toung. He passed in a ravine that led to a branch of Deer Creek. We lost sight

---

great piles, many chords of it—good meat. Bags of beans, salt, &c. &c. Trunks, chests, tools of every description, clothing, tents, tent-poles, harness, &c. &c." After noting that trains of ox wagons were coming up hourly, he wrote that "at Deer Creek there is a camp of 3 wagons & several Missourians, who have two wagons heavily laden with Alcohol, for California. This they dilute, and with dried apples, peaches, &c. manufacture all kinds of liquors." See Read and Gaines, eds., *Gold Rush*, I, 45–47.

of him and it being near night we could not find him in time
to return to camp. We struck the creek five miles above the
mouth of the creek. We started down the stream. It was
dark and comeing across a party hurding cattle we staid with
them over night. Distance traveled 25 miles.

July 13

We moved up the creek about 8 miles to recruit our animals and to cut some hay. We found a beautiful camping
place where the grass is quite good, into which our mules
plunged and refreshed themselves after their privation.
Several of us proceeded up a small branch and cut some hay.
We found some *praire hens* or sage hens, 5 of which we shot.
Buffalo, Elk, Deer, Antelope and other game are quite
plentiful. There are many rumors of scarcity of food, and
marauding parties, &c calculated to frighten the timid but
all of our company keep up good courage and seem determined to put it through at all hazards.

[Staples]

This morning Whittier and I returned to our party.
Found them camped near the crossing of the river. We
moved up the creek six miles to stop a day or two for our
mules to rest, and [to] cut some hay. We camped near a
fork in the creek, a grand place. Fair grass. We mowed some
hay, enough to give our mules a lunch for a few days. Today
some of our men shot several ducks. I shot four prara hens
and if nothing happens we will have a rich dinner tomorrow.

July 14

We remained encamped today to refresh the animals and
make our hay. Nothing of importance transpired worthy
of note.[6]

---

[6] Back in Walpole, Massachusetts, Major Gould wrote in his journal:
"Received information that my son, Charles, had a son born on the 14th of
July, while Betsey, the mother was in Hartland, Maine, and Charles on his
way to California."

135

[Staples]

This day has been spent in shoeing mules, making hay &c. We have had a glorious dinner, a regular fowl soup—delicious. Since we have been here we have had as much milk as we wanted of parties hurding their cattle near us.

Sunday, July 15

We left the ground early this morning for the ferry situated about half a mile from where the regular trail crosses Deer Creek. The river is a[bout] 800 ft. wide here with a swift current. The boats are constructed of 6 *dug outs* fastened together and worked by oars. It took us until 4 P.M. to get them across—the animals were swam across. We then passed over a very sandy road and a very bad hill and encamped in a beautiful grove where the feed was pretty good upon the banks of the river.

[Staples]

Today we have crossed the Platte again, being ferryed across by a party from Ill. who, on coming up to the ferry, found it governed by a *Mormon* who was asking $2.50 for ferrying over a waggon.

They went to work and made a raft of logs dug out. They ferryed us over for .50 cts a waggon. This had the right effect to make him reduce his fare the same. We had to swim our mules over. We got all safely over and started at four o'clock over a hilly, sandy road. We camped on the banks of the river in a pleasant grove, some grass. We are all well enough today to ride on horseback. (Distance from the old camp up to the creek 10 miles.)

July 16

Our road today has been very sandy and severe for the animals. In some places they were completely stalled, which exhausted the animals very much. We travelled until half past nine and encamped where the trail from the upper

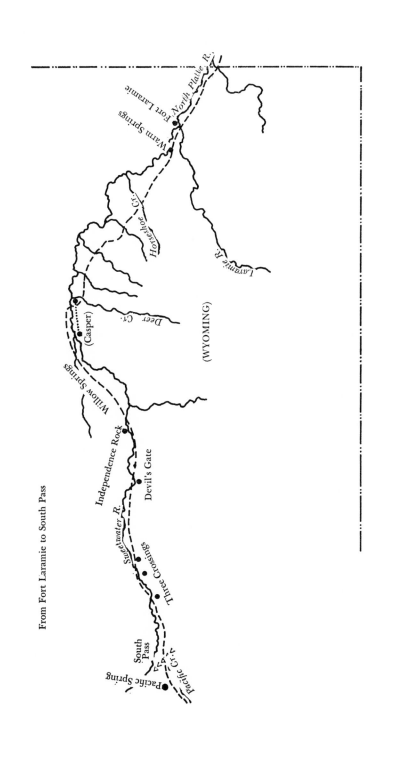

From Fort Laramie to South Pass

ferry[7] unites with this. There was no grass here and we were obliged to feed out of our hay to them. We threw away about 6 or 8 hundred lbs. weight of pack together with the India Rubber boat to lighten the loads.

[Staples]

This morning we moved at six o'clock and the hardest road we have had. Very soft sand Bluffs. We have all heavy loads today, haveing one waggon for hay and buying yesterday at the crossing hard bread and rice to the amt. of four hundred pounds. We halted at noon on the river. Some little grass. Has the appearance of haveing been mowed, the head teems eat it so close. We had a meeting today noon to see about light[en]ing our loads. We concluded to leave all but 500 *lbs.* of our pork, finding we did not consume near as much as was estimated. We left it beside the road for all that need it. We concluded to part with 75 lbs of coffee and all that could be spared. We moved late this evening, camped on a sand Bluff, and found our hay most valuable. Distance 18 miles.

July 17

We passed over a steep hill which was very tedious as the sand was very deep. It fatigued the animals more than a day's work. 8 miles from the camp the road takes its final leave of the Platte to strike the Sweetwater—It passes through a dreary, desolate looking country[8] destitute of vegitation, but it is hard and smooth. We encamped upon a small grassy spot which afforded a decent allowance of grass.

[Staples]

This forenoon our road was more hilly and sandy. We left the river at 11 o'clock for good. Halted in a valley four miles beyond. The teams had to labor so hard that quite a number called a meeting to make arrangements for packing

---

[7] The ferry was located near present Casper, Wyoming.
[8] Dams were built later on, creating lakes in this area.

the company. The majority voted not to pack but try it a day or two longer. This afternoon the road has been better. We have passed today some hard hills. We camped tonight on the banks of a small creek. Found a spring; some *alkali* taste to the water. No wood but wild sage. Distance 20 miles.

July 18

The trail has been quite good today. The water is so strongly impregnated with alkali, salt and sulpher that we dare not let our animals drink much of it. We have passed 64 dead oxen in the last 3 days, 34 of which we passed today. Their deaths are mostly caused by being overworked and by drinking of the impure waters. We passed a beautiful spring this afternoon where the refreshing waters were truly a luxury to our parched and thirsty lips. We next passed over an elevated dividing ridge from the top of which we had a view of the Sweetwater Mountain. The scenery in all directions was exceedingly picturesque and beautiful. We were so fortunate as to find a good camping place in a small hollow where there was a spring of clear, cold water.

[Staples]

Today we started early with a view of getting to a spring 14 miles distant. We pased (Rock Avanue) this morning, but the road has been generally quite good. We halted at noon near the spring and creek. No grass. We fed out the rest of our hay here as we found no grass.

This afternoon we passed "Willow Spring," a spring of as cold water as man ever tasted. After leaving the spring we ascended a verry high hill. Here we had a most glorious view of the mountain scenery. We camped near a spring and good grass. This was the best camp we have enjoyed for some time. Distance 20 miles.

July 19

The weather is very cold this morning. The road has been very sandy and heavy the most of the way. We passed several alkali lakes, some of which were encrusted ½ an inch thick with pure carbonate of soda. We did not stop at noon owing to the scarcity of grass, but drove until 4 when we encamped upon the banks of the Sweetwater. One of our wagons was knocked to pieces and burnt here owing to the bad condition into which it had got. We passed 25 dead oxen and 1 mule.

[Staples]

Today we have had a verry hard sandy road. We pased this morning a fine running stream and at 11 o'clock we came to a succession of lakes crusted over with alkalie. Some of them near a half inch thick—some places more than others. We halted on the rise after passing these lakes for the teams to come up. We moved after an hour's halt and four miles brought us to the (Sweetwater). We hailed it with delight. Found a good place to camp and halted for the night near the Independance Rock, a place where every passerby leaves his signature. Distance 16 miles.

July 20

1 mile from our camp was Independence Rock,[9] an isolated mass of granite, 120 feet high and 2000 feet long. It is covered wherever there is room with names of travellers. 5 miles farther is the Devil's Gate, where the Sweet-Water makes its passage through a fissure in the mountain walls; it is 35 yds. wide and 300 yds. long. Its walls are perpendicular and about 400 ft. high. We found good grass for our animals' dinner and most excellent for one night's encampment. The road has been pretty good though rather sandy. We camped at 6 in a bend of the river.

---

[9] "The rock was a landmark and an ingenious post office. Emigrants left their names, dates, and sometimes messages. Presumably it was named Independence Rock by [William] Ashley's men who camped there on July 4, 1825. Father De Smet saw so many names and messages on the rock in 1840, that he called it 'The Register of the West.'" Velma Linford, *Wyoming: Frontier State* (Denver: Old West Publishing Co., 1947), p. 101.

[Staples]

Today our road has been mostly along the Banks of the river, occasionally strikeing across the Bluffs. These are soft sand and verry hard for teems to get through. At 11 o'clock our road ran near the upper side of the "Devils Gate," [as] an opening in the Mountains for the river to run through the cut is called by the Mormon guide.[10] 400 feet perpendicular and 80 feet wide, it looked like the passageway of some higher power. Anyway it is one of those wonders of nature that man likes to admire. The "Sweetwater" Ridge must be a part of the Rocky Mountains as they are a solid rock. No herbage but an occasional stunted Cedar in some crevice.

We camp tonight on the banks of the river 17 miles from our last camp.

"Today we have disposed of one of our waggons making our remaining loads rather heavy."[11] "For a week past we have passed a large number of Ox trains. The hard chance we have had for grass has compelled them to give out, many of them. We find them along the road oftener than every mile, and parties with them have to lay by to recruit the remaining one."

July 21

We remain encamped today to recruit our animals and to cut off 2 of our wagons which are decided to be too long. Nothing of particular importance has occurred today.

---

[10] According to note 15 in Taggart, "The Journal of David Jackson Staples," p. 149: "The 'Mormon Guide' was undoubtedly William Clayton's *The Latter-Day Saints' Emigrants' Guide: Being a Table of Distances, Showing All the Springs, Creeks, Rivers, Hills, Mountains, Camping Places . . . from Council Bluffs to the Valley of the Great Salt Lake . . .* (St. Louis, 1848). The reference to Devil's Gate is on p. 15. Clayton prepared the guide from his own observations and the record of Orson Pratt's roadometer."

[11] There is no apparent reason for the use of quotation marks around statements in this paragraph. Perhaps Staples just felt like putting them in.

140

[Staples]

Today we have laid by to give our mules a chance to recruit. We found it expedient to improve some of our waggons by shortening the body. We find others have done it with good results. All well and everything ready for an early start.

Sunday, July 22

We got away as the sun was rising. The road has been very sandy and heavy today. The valley of the Sweet Water is about 10 or 12 miles wide, bordered on both sides by mountains rising from 1 to 2000 ft. in height. Those on the left bank are bare granite rocks entirely destitute of vegetation excepting a few hardy pines which obtain a hold in the crevices and wherever a little earth is collected. The river sweeps near their base. Those on the right bank seem to be covered by trees and other vegetation. There was a severe thunder shower this afternoon which settled the sand together and made it easier travelling. A buffalo passed near us at noon, but we missed shooting him. We came across a man this afternoon who had got lost from a party that were crossing from *Santa Fe* to this trail—he had been 4 days without food and was very much exhausted.

[Staples]

This morning we were moveing at five. Our road lay mostly along the river banks; some hard sand Bluffs to cross. We halted at noon on the river, 10 miles from our camp yesterday. While here a Buffalo came down to drink a little above our camp. The camp was soon roused and the rifles read[y]. A dozen men started on foot to cut him off. They returned in an hour only getting one shot at him. This afternoon a man came to us who got lost four days before on a hunting excursion. He looked miserable, haveing nothing to eat for four days. We fed him and he is with us tonight. He proves to be a regular Phys[ician] from *Miss*, belonging to a pack mule party. This afternoon we have had a real

141

shower, the first we have had for 35 days. It was a great relief to the dust. We camped tonight near the crossing of the river under a mountain of rocks. Good grass and wood. Distance 19 miles.

July 23

We have crossed the river 4 times today.[12] The road has been much less sandy and much easier. Owing to the distance to the river, we were obliged to travel until past 9 in order to reach it, it having [been?] to the right of the trail several miles. The mountains on our right have settled into bluffs of sand. We had the first sight of the Wind River Mountains, the top of which are white with snow. We have passed as many as 30 dead oxen today and I think that the average for the last 4 or 5 days has been 25 per day. As we were obliged to [be?] camping in the night we were so unfortunate as to have but little or no grass. We made 28 miles today.

[Staples]

This morning our road for the first three miles was directly through the mountains, crossing the river three times in a mile or two.

At half past ten we traveled up a rise and the first sight that attracted our notice was the Mountains ahead covered with snow. They were supposed to be the "Wind River" *Mts* north of the South Pass. We made our noon halt at a crossing in the river and learned we had to travel 16 miles before comeing to the river again. No grass between the two points. We pushed for it. Came to the river at 10 o'clock P.M. Mules and men hartily tired, haveing traveled 28 miles on short feed. The air this evening is quite cold, being like our evenings the last of September. Here at the

---

[12] In this part of the journey along the Sweetwater the river made three sharp bends in the ever ascending plain. The famous Three Crossings came in rapid succession and slowed down the caravans.

crossing we found several trains of ox teems and learned the great *Pass* was within two days drive. Some parties here had lost their whole teems by a stampede.

July 24

We did not travel but 6 miles today on account of the great distance we traveled yesterday and the distance we shall have to go to get to another camping place. We encamped at 10 upon the banks of the river and although the grass was quite short, the mules soon satisfied themselves. Mr. Norris of the Granite State and Mt. Washington Company came into camp today in pursuit of 4 deserters from Ft. Kearny, who had perpetrated outrages upon some emigrants. They stayed at our camp last night and are now pushing ahead.

[Staples]

This morning we moved on up the river. Passed over a verry high rise, as much of a mountain as we have passed over. Struck the river some six miles above our last camp. Here we found a party leaveing a waggon. We obtained it for wood, and camped for the day to rest our teems etc.

July 25

Water froze in the buckets last night to the thickness of window glass. My thermometer was 30°. We started in good season with a beautiful, clear atmosphere. We left the Sweet Water and crossed over some very high hills, the tops of which were very rocky and dangerous to the wagons; the rest of the road was more level. After travelling 14 miles, we nooned in a small ravine known as Strawberry Creek, but the grass was very poor.

Capt. Duncan[13] arrived in pursuit of the deserters spoken of yesterday. We made 10 miles more this afternoon over a

---

[13] Captain Thomas Duncan served in the Mounted Riflemen, which was made up of ten companies. The Act of Congress passed in 1846 authorizing

beautiful road and encamped for the last time upon the delightful Sweet Water. Capt. D[uncan] and assistant staid with us tonight.

[Staples]

This morning the water in our pails near the campfire were frozen over, an indication that we were on a good deal of an elevation. We passed up the banks of the Sweetwater some five miles. Our road then struck over the hills and verry high and hard compared to any we have passed. We halted at noon on Strawberry Creek. While here *Capt* Duncan of the Mounted rifle men came in to camp. We invited him to diner. We learned he was in persuit of four deserters from his Company who had run from Fort Larime. Besides taking horses and arms belonging to the Company they robed an emigrant of two hundred dollars and ravaged his wife. He kept company with us this afternoon. His horse [was] nearly given out. He offered $100 to our party to send on a man or men to catch them. We had no horses that it would do to send. We passed this afternoon two fine creeks, both tributaries to the Sweetwater. We camped tonight near the last crossing of the river. Distance traveled 24 miles.

July 26

We took our final leave of the Sweet Water this morning and after travelling 9 miles up a very gentle ascent we reached the South Pass. We could hardly believe that we stood upon

---

the Riflemen appropriated $76,500 for mounting and equipping the troops. Companies C and E, commanded by Major Winslow F. Sanderson, arrived at Fort Laramie on June 27, 1849. Company E, which was led by Captain Duncan, was made up of five officers and fifty-eight men. See Hafen and Young, *Fort Laramie and the Pageant of the West, 1834–1890*, pp. 138–142, and *Publications of the Nebraska State Historical Society*, XX (1922), 192. According to Bruff's journal, the "assistant" that Gould mentions is Stinson, who guided his party across the plains, then enlisted as a teamster at Cantonment Loring, a post near Fort Hall. See Read and Gaines, eds., *Gold Rush*, entries for May 2, July 25, and August 20.

the dividing ridge between the Atlantic and Pacific Oceans. It seemed more like a rolling Praire, and in the north can be seen the Wind River Mts. with their tops covered with snow. They are all of the mountains visible from the Pass.[14] The soil is sandy and barren, covered mostly with wild sage. Three miles down a very gentle descent brought us to the Pacific Spring, a very large and cold spring whose waters flow into the Gulf of California. There being pretty good feed here, we encamped for the rest of the day.

[Staples]

We had Capt. Duncan stay with us last night. This morning he got several of our men to accompany him a few miles, hopeing to come up with the men he was in persuit of. We started late, intending to travel only 14 miles to Pacific Spring. 9 miles from camp we passed the turning point in the Mountains. The road has been good today and the rise verry little. We began to decend and three miles further brought us to Pacific Springs. Good grass and fine water. We arrived at one o'clock. Camped for the day. Distance 12 miles.

---

[14] "On the north and south sides of the pass, snow-covered mountain peaks cut the sky; within it rose two streams. That which flowed to the east ultimately discharged its waters in the Gulf of Mexico; the west-running stream emptied into the Pacific Ocean." Lola M. Homsher, ed., *South Pass, 1868: James Chisholm's Journal of the Wyoming Gold Rush* (Lincoln: University of Nebraska Press, 1960), p. 3. Because it was south of other trails previously used only by mounted men, it came to be called South Pass.

CHAPTER 9

South Pass to Salt Lake City

After South Pass there was a marked change in the character of the road west. On the plains as many as six or more lanes ran parallel with one another, but on mountain trails there frequently was but one narrow path. Moreover, the difficulty and monotony of the journey often frayed the nerves of men who were normally good-tempered, and even as well balanced, civilized, and resolute a group as the Boston-Newton company was not exempt from clashes between its members.

July 27

Our road [Gould wrote] led over very sterile and barren soil today, the growth of which is chiefly wild sage which together with the sandy soil gives a dull greyish tint to the landscape.

We halted at noon where there was no grass, but we had the good fortune to have a little corn left [carried from Independence], 1 pint of which was dealt out to each animal, which in a measure relieved their hunger and gave them courage to finish their day's labor. We arrived at the Little Sandy 25 miles from the Pacific Spring just before sundown, but much to our regret found the grass entirely gone. We therefore had to picket our mules amongst the wild sage and let them pick out such as best they could.

147

[Staples]

This morning we made an early start, having learned by our guide that it was 24 miles to the next water and grass.[1] Our road has been some decending, generally level, more so than I anticipated. No herbage except wild sage and occasionally a bunch of greese wood. We halted at noon and baited our mules on corn we had with us. The road has been much harder today than usual. We arrived at sunset on our camp ground on the banks of the Little Sandy. A fine stream 15 ft. wide, cold Water comeing right from the Mountains. No grass and little wood. Distance 25 miles.

July 28

I was on guard the latter part of the night, but the poor mules made such mournful complaint that I roused the cooks and breakfast was over and we were on our way at half past four. At 7½ we arrived at *Big Sandy where we proceeded 1 mile up stream and found a bountiful supply of grass for our hungry animals.

17 miles farther down down stream we encamped on the same stream. The grass was fed pretty close, but our animals done very well. My team was about 1 mile behind the rest and 1 of the tires came off, which delayed [me] still longer so I did not get into camp until 9.

* Big Sandy is the river which we nooned on.

[Staples]

This morning we were off before sunrise. We arrived on the banks of the Big Sandy, eight miles from the Little.

---

[1] According to a footnote in Harold F. Taggart, ed., "The Journal of David Jackson Staples," p. 149: "The Mormon Guide, under 'Pacific creek (crossing)' remarks: 'After you leave here you will find a good road, but very little water.' Of the Dry Sandy, nine miles farther on, the Guide said: 'The water brackish, and not good for cattle. Very little grass, but no wood.' Six miles beyond that came the 'Junction of the California and Oregon roads. Take the left hand road.' And it was 7¾ more miles to the Little Sandy."

Found good grass, grazed our mules till noon. While here we shot several sage hens and hares, furnishing us meat for soup. Today we have passed several large trains of ox teems. We find on this, the *Mormon Road, better* traveling than we expected. The wind has been verry strong today and cold, so much so that an overcoat is not uncomfortable. We camped tonight on the Big Sandy, 25 miles from our last camp and ten miles to the *Colorad* or Green River.[2]

Sunday, July 29

We reached the ferry on Green River 10 miles from our last night's camp, at 10½. The river is about 200 ft. wide with a strong, swift current. The ferry is owned by the Mormons and was established to accommodate the Mormon emigrants—the fare is $2 per wagon. The mules are driven about ¾ of a mile up the river where it is not so steep and can across. We [met] Capt. Duncan with the 4 deserters, which he had caught at this place and which he intended to take back to Ft. Larimie, making them perform the whole journey on foot. After we had crossed, we went down stream 4 miles and encamped with good wood, water, and grass.

[Staples]

We determined to move onto the Green River to find better grass. We arrived river at Eleven o'clock, found it hard to ford. Hired a Mormon to ferry us over at $2 a wagon. This is a beautifull stream, 200 yards wide, swift current and clear water. We moved down the river four miles and camped on its banks. Good grass and plenty of timber and it is a great relief to the barron country we have passed over since we left the Platte.

---

[2] The Green River, which discharges into the Colorado River, rises in the Rockies in present Wyoming. It was known to the Spaniards as the Rio Verde and to the Crow Indians as the Siskadee.

At the ferry we came up with Captain Duncan who left us three days before. He found his four deserters at this place. Poor fellows, they are to be pitied. Distance 13 miles.

July 30

Having become tired of driving team so long, I resigned and Mr. Loring took it. I made my first appearance upon mule back and a very tiresome job it was. We turned our animals amongst some bunch grass which is quite dry, but affords excellent nourishment for the mules, who eat it with great avidity. We stopped on Blacks Fork of Green River, where the grass was excellent, having made 25 miles today.

[Staples]

This morning for three miles our road lay along the banks of the Green River, and after traveling over a barron country for a month such a change as this a great relief. The banks are well wooded and the green lawns present a most grattifying picture. After leaving the river we struck over the bluffs and for 17 miles the country is more roling than a few days back. We struck a fine stream. Black fk. We passed on after wattering and camped four miles beyond on Maders Creek. Good grass, no wood, but willows. Distance 25 miles. While we were haveing our nooning a most brutal affair took place between two of our members, "White and Ayer." It commenced by White pushing Ayer and kicking him. In return Ayer threw a hatchet he held in his hand at the time. It struck White on the thy and cut a gash four inches long, quite deep. Men get cross sometimes on this trip and haveing all restraint thrown off they act rash. I hope we shall not have another case of assault. It lowers us in the eyes of other Companies and ourselves.

July 31

1 mile from Blacks Fork we crossed Hams Fork, a beautiful clear stream. 1 mile farther we crossed Blacks

Fork. The road has been very good today and we encamped upon Blacks Fork, where the grass was excellent.

[Staples]

We moved early. Crossed the creek we camped on, pased over a more roling country. This forenoon we met the Mormon express[3] going back to the states. They informed us that considerable of the *gold* from *Cal* had arrived at the settlement. We learned that we could get vegetables etc at the Salt Lake. This was good news to us. Our road ran along near the "Rain Bow" bluffs. They derive their name from the different colours of clay and sand mixed up the sides. We noticed one prominent Bluff whose sides presented with a little strech of imagination every variety of forms—groups of men, heads of animals &c. Looked like Egiptian architecture. We halted at noon on Black's Fork. Good grass. This afternoon we saw several antelope. Shot some sage hens and one hare, which furnished us good material for a soup. We camped on a creek of rapid running water, cold and clear, comeing from the Utaw Mountains whose peaks are ever covered with snow, makeing the nights cold and needing overcoats in the morning.

August 1

We left our camp bright and early. 8 miles brought us to Ft. Bridger,[4] a private trading post carried on by Messrs. Bridger and Vasquez who trade with the Indians for furs and skins. The Ft. is built of logs, composing a hollow square about 100 feet on each side.

---

[3] "The Mormons established their own stage and express from the Missouri border" (Frederic L. Paxson, *History of the American Frontier* [Boston: Houghton Mifflin Co., 1924], p. 461.

[4] Fort Bridger, built in 1842 by the famous mountain man Jim Bridger (1804–1881), was described by him thus in a letter to a St. Louis merchant: "I have established a small fort, with a blacksmith shop and a supply of iron in the road of the emigrants which promises fairly. In coming out here they are generally well supplied with money but by the time they get here they are in need of all kinds of supplies, horses, provisions, smith work, etc. . . .

There was a tribe of Soshones or Snake Indians[5] encamped near the Ft. They seemed to have enough to eat and wear but their filth was very disgusting. As we had determined to go by the way of the Mormon City, we took the left hand trail, the right hand going by way of Ft. Hall.[6] The road had a gradual rise for several miles when it descended into a valley by a very steep and stony hill which was very dangerous for the teams. We encamped upon a small creek known as Muddy creek.

[Staples]

Mr. Noyse is quite sick this morning of an attack of Mountain fever.[7] We moved on at 7 o'clock, thinking to

---

The fort is a beautiful location on Black's Fork of Green River, receiving fine fresh water from the snow on the Unitah Range. The streams are alive with mountain trout. It passes the fort in several channels, each lined with trees, kept alive by the moisture of the soil." Quoted in Howard R. Driggs, *The Old West Speaks* (Englewood, N.J.: Prentice-Hall, Inc., 1956), p. 41. In 1849 Captain Howard Stansbury reported to the War Department: "[The fort] is built in the usual form of pickets, with lodging apartment and offices opening into a hollow square, protected from without by a strong gate of timber. On the north and continuous with the wall is a strong picket fence enclosing a large yard, into which the animals belonging to the establishment are driven for protection from wild beasts and Indians." Quoted in Linford, *Wyoming: Frontier State*, p. 126.

5 The Shoshonis were the most northerly division of the Shoshonean family; they formerly occupied parts of Wyoming, Idaho, Nevada, and Utah, with their stronghold in the Snake River country of Idaho. In 1805 Lewis and Clark encountered the northern bands at the headwaters of the Missouri in western Montana. Although Gould refers to them here as the "Snake Indians," the term "seems to have no etymological connection with the designation Shoshoni." See F. W. Hodge, ed., *Handbook of American Indians North of Mexico* (New York: Pageant Books, Inc., 1959), II, 557.

6 Fort Hall, located near the juncture of the Snake and Portneuf rivers in present Idaho, was built in 1834.

7 An undiagnosed illness that appeared among travelers on the overland trails in the 1840's and 1850's mostly after they reached the high altitudes. There are numerous references to mountain fever in accounts of trail travel of the 1840's through the 1860's.

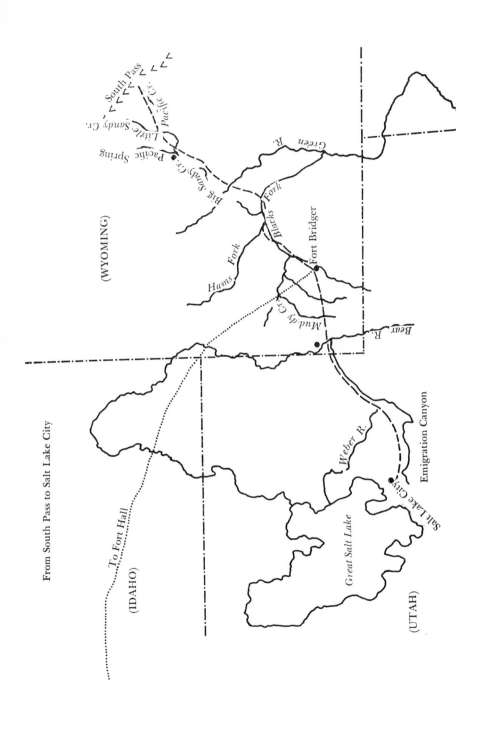

From South Pass to Salt Lake City

stop at "Fort Bridger" eight miles from our last camp. Arrived at the fort at 10 o'clock. Near the fort we passed three rapid runing streams. Within a half mile of the Fort on the Banks of these streams was a large number of Indian wigwams, most of them Sosone or Snake. Quite a large number came to us and by signes asked for bread. We gave them and they still beged. It seamed as though there was no sattisfying their hunger. Poorly clad. The man lazeing about and the Squas at home working hard dressing skins. Here we found several traders who had most of them Indian wives, and you could see in the little pappoose crawling about the blood of the white man. The indians were remarkably civel. No one of them showed any disposition to steal. We paid a visit to the Fort.

It is built of logs and quite a comfortable place to stay. After our halt we moved on, and our road was over high hills and part of the Utaw Mts. After 12 miles traveling over the hills, a splendid valley appears below some two miles. We found a fine stream and pretty good grass, some wood. We camped well sattisfied. Our sick man some better. Distance 22 miles.

August 2

An Indian came into our camp [last night] to trade horses and as we wished to examine his by daylight we kept him until morning when the trade was concluded. We passed over a high dividing ridge which separates the waters between the Colorado and the Great Basin.

We passed the Bear River just before night and encamped about 1 mile from it. This is a large, clear and beautiful stream which empties into Salt Lake after a circuitous route, its course being north here.

The grass tonight is excellent and the mules seem happy and contented. There was a small party of Snakes encamped on the river near the ford.

[Staples]

Our road this morning lay over high hills. After traveling up three or four miles we had a tedious decent. Road rocky. Nothing of note except mountain scenery, which is grand. The snow-covered peaks on one hand and the thousand streams runing from them with an occasional raviene with a grove of pople [poplar] to releive the mind. We find the mornings verry cold here. Ice quite often is found in our watter buckets.

We made our noon halt on the side of one of the highest peaks we have passed. After passing this ridge our road decended into a most beautiful valley. After winding about the hill, we struck across another ridge and had a fine view of Bear River and Valley from the hill. Our road was verry steep and stoney for a mile, which brought us to the river—a fine stream of three rods wide, rapid current. We did not find grass here sufficient to stop, having been well grazed by party and indians. Here we found two lodges of the Snake Indians. These fellows beat all for begging. We passed on over the first ridge and camped. Plenty of grass, no water or wood. Distance 22 miles.

August 3

After passing over another high hill, we entered a narrow ravine bounded on one side by perpendicular walls of red sandstone of great height and on the other mountains of earth of equal height. I believe it is called Echo Valley, owing to the walls causing sound to reverbrate a great deal. We encamped tonight in the ravine in as romantic a place as the greatest fancier of nature could wish.

[Staples]

This morning we were off in good season. We had a good road—somewhat hilly the first part and then by a pleasant decent we found ourselves in a splendid valley. We found a good spring, this four miles from our last camp. The edges were frozen over. The air is quite cold. This morning we followed down this valley and small stream four miles and struck across the ridge into another valley by a long and tedious decent. We halted at noon near a spring of cold water. Good grass. This was 15 miles from the river. Here we found two more lodges numbering in all twenty. They persued the course of all we have passed—*beg.* We gave them and they seemed eqully dissatisfied. Want more. They are of a smaller size than those we met in the first part of the trip and miserably poor. Soon after noon we struck into an echo valley and followed it till night, crossing a small stream in it several times. Towards night the hills grew higher and squarer, three or four hundred feet perpendicular, and the ravine where we crossed more dangerous. We camped to-night near the stream. Poor grass. Distance 28 miles.

August 4

8 or 10 miles carried us through the valley when we struck Weber Creek, a beautiful mountain stream which empties into the Great Salt Lake. We followed this 4 miles when we turned up another ravine and encamped.

[Staples]

This forenoon we still followed the valley, often crossing the stream. Saw some splendid views. On one side perpendicular Bluffs several hundred feet high. On the other the side hills covered with grass and herbage. I noticed today some shrub oaks, the first I have seen. At noon we struck "Webbers" river, a fine stream. We halted a mile below where we struck it. Grass rather poor, plenty of wood on it. We passed party of Mormans today, and obtained of them milk and *Butter*, the latter the first we have had since leaveing the States and as great a luxury as could be offered to us. We forded the river three miles below our noon halt. Passed on the hills into a ravine two miles from the river and camped for the night. Distance 12 miles.

Sunday, August 5

A few miles brought us to Kanyon Creek, which we have crossed a great many times. The road has been very hard for the animals and we did not make but 11 miles. We are encamped in the ravine and drove the animals up the bank where the grass was quite good. The road to the settlement is said to be very mountainous and hard.

[Staples]

Today we have had a hard road, passing up a narrow ravine most of the way on the side hills. Quite dangerous, crossing a creek near a dozen times. One of our teems got upset in a bad place. We came up with a large party of forty Waggons. Ox teems. We followed them within a mile of the road, leaving the river, and camped for the night. Distance 12 miles.

August 6

We passed over a high mountain which was very difficult to ascend and descend. It was very cold on the top from which we had a splendid prospect of the mountains to the South West. We also had a view of the great valley, which did not look but a few miles distant.

[Staples]

Today our road after a mile from camp turned to the right up a Kenyon. We followed it some four miles up, often crossing a small gulley with some water. This Kenyon was well timbered. It led us on a verry prominent peak of the range, the decent of which was exceedingly steep and dangerous. We followed it down four miles and many times crossing a rapid runing creek. Near a dozen times. We camped at the foot of the last hill (rightly called Mountain) that separates us from the Salt Lake Valley. Today we have had the best view of mountain scenery that has greeted us on the trip. We descended the hill without accident and well sattisfied with our day's work.

156

August 7

After passing over another mountain and passing through a ravine for several miles, we entered the valley, when we had a view of the great *Salt Lake,* which did not look but a few miles distant although it was 25. The City looked like a garden with tents scattered about it, as we looked down upon it from the heights.[8]

We passed through the City and encamped at the western side upon the unoccupied land. Our mules were put under the care of a young man, who took them out several miles where the feed was more plentiful. I took dinner at a private house, where we enjoyed the luxuries of a vegetable dinner.

We all feel much relieved to find a place where we can rest a while.

[Staples]

This morning for a mile our road lay up a steep hill. On arriving at the top we halted for a while, then decended a sharp pitch into a ravine with a rapid runing stream of cold water. After crossing the stream 19 times brought us in full view of the Valley and a more beautifull sight could not be presented to our view. Hundreds of acres of corn, wheat, and vegetables. We moved through the main street [of Salt Lake City] and camped on what is called the Commons, outside the city fence. We gave our mules over to the herdsman for a few days and prepared ourselves to enjoy the good things of the Valley for a few days. Distance traveled today 12 miles.

August 8

The city is laid out into regular squares, 40 rods on each side. These are divided into lots of 1¼ acre each, which are

[8] It was on July 24, 1847, that the Mormon vanguard, led by Brigham Young, emerged from what came to be called Emigration Canyon and looked down into the valley. "Brigham Young, ill with mountain fever, . . . rose from his bed [in a wagon], looked over the scene, and said, 'This is the place!'" Driggs, *The Old West Speaks,* p. 103.

drawn for by lot by the residents who have no right to sell them but are inherited by their followers. The streets are 8 rods in width. The city is about 2 miles square. As no rain falls in the summer, the gardens and farms are watered by irrigation. The streams which run down from the mountains are conducted over the city by trenches and each person has his regular allowance.

The houses are mostly built of sun burnt brick or, as people call them, *dobys*, which are made by mixing the earth with water and moulding them into the same manner as common bricks are moulded, and then drying them in the sun for about 2 weeks—they are said to very durable in this climate.

All of the houses have been put up since last fall, excepting those which are in the fort which are to be pulled down, as they do not conform to the regular plan of the city, they having been put up as temporary residences for the protection of the first pioneers, who first came in the summer of 1847. The inhabitants are representatives from all parts of the world who are collected here to enjoy their peculiar views of religion &c. They seem to be happy and contented with the situation, the earth yielding them a sufficient amount for their subsistence.

The Great Salt Lake lies 25 miles west of the city and affords them an abundant supply of salt free of cost. The Utah Lake lies 20 or 30 miles south of this and is connected to it by a stream, which the inhabitants call the *Jordan*. There is no animal life in the Salt Lake, but the Utah is said to abound with Salmon trout, which affords the entire subsistence of the Indians who live upon its borders. The Utah Mts. border the valley to the east, the tops of which are covered with perpetual snow, presenting scenery of great beauty. We here decided to leave our wagons and pack our animals in order to facilitate our progress in the remaining part of our journey. Accordingly pack saddles were ordered.

Our wagons were sold and everyone was busy preparing for
our new mode of travel. We have all enjoyed ourselves very
much here, finding plenty of fresh vegetables, butter, milk,
&c. to feast upon, and resting after our laborious travelling
across the mountains.

[Staples]

Today we have looked about the city for information
respecting the wisest way to finish our trip and have decided
to pack our mules and shove through and have made arrangements for our packs and disposed of some of our waggons
in exchange.

Today our party took dinner with *Mr. Ira J. Williss,* one
of the Mormon battallion who was in *Cal* on the discovery
of gold. His brother was in the trench to work for **Sutter**
when the discovery was made. *Ira* gave us some verry grattifying inteligence of the abundance of the *filthy lucre.* We
shall be better sattisfied when we see for ourselves.

CHAPTER 10

Salt Lake City to the Humboldt River

In the course of the journey from Massachusetts, the Boston-Newton company had made use of three modes of transportation —trains, steamboats, and covered wagons. From Salt Lake City on, they would travel by pack mule. Each man was assigned two animals: one to ride and one to pack. The company also took along seven extra mules, and the officers still rode horseback when they left Salt Lake City.

It was a tricky business to pack the equipment to be carried and to load the huge packs on the backs of the mules. First, a heavy blanket was placed on the back of the mule; then the pack saddle was put on and cinched up tightly. Generally the baggage was wrapped and tied in a canvas cover before it was secured to the saddle. It took practice to learn how to adjust the loads so that the packs would not shake loose and to make sure that the backs of the mules would not get sore.

Three trails from Salt Lake crossed the region called the Great Basin, which extends from Salt Lake to the Sierra Nevada range. One led westward over the salt flats on the south side of the lake to the Humboldt. The second took a northwesterly course to Fort Hall and then turned south toward the City of Rocks, a point thirty miles north of the boundary line of present Idaho. From the City of Rocks it continued toward the south to meet the

Humboldt near its source, and this waterway directed the course of the trail through the territory that is now Nevada. The third route, called the Salt Lake Cutoff, had been pioneered in 1848.[1] From Bear River, eighty miles north of Salt Lake City, this trail took a westerly course across the northern portion of what is now Utah to meet the California-Oregon trail near City of Rocks, also called Steeple Rocks.

The Salt Lake Cutoff was the route chosen by the Boston-Newton company, and it took them ten days, until August 24, to reach the old road. As in the preceding chapters, Gould's account is presented first in the day-to-day narration of the journey.

August 15

After considerable delay, a few of us started and made our first appearance on pack mules. 1 mile from the city is a beautiful warm sulphur spring which is much used by the inhabitants for bathing. The temperature is 103°.

2 miles farther is another, which is hotter than a person can hold their hand in.

The road is very level and easy to travel.

After travelling 10 miles, we came to a small, clear creek, near which we encamped for the night. At 11 in the night, 4 more of our number came in. There is a number of farm houses near by.

[Staples]

After a week's sojourn with the Mormons we leave today with regrets, haveing received the kindest attention from all we have had to do with. On the tenth we pitched our *Marque[e]* tent and invited Elder Taylor[2] to address us on

---

[1] For information about the Salt Lake Cutoff, which was discovered in August, 1848, by Samuel J. Hensley, returning to California from Washington, D.C., see L. A. Fleming and A. R. Standing, "The Salt Lake Cutoff," *Utah Historical Society Quarterly* (1966), pp. 248–271.

[2] A former Methodist minister, John Taylor became a famed Mormon missionary and apostle and eventually president of the Mormon Church.

the general items that constitute the Mormon creed. He spoke to us in verry plain talk of the treatment they received in the States, and wo be to those men that were active in the persecution if they ever enter the City. [Staples later recalled that they had "quite a congregation" when the Boston-Newton company "listened for the first time in our lives to Mormon ideas. Taylor made one remark that struck the Boston ears as rather peculiar. He said, 'You gentlemen, who come from New England, who have not been identified with the men who have persecuted the saints, are welcome here, and the city and all that we have is at your service, but if those men who persecuted the saints should come into Salt Lake City, we would send them to hell crosslots.' That was part of his sermon. . . ."³] We were visited in our stay by *President Young*, their leading prophet (for they beleive in *prophets* and *Bishops* and all the ancient organization of society). He seemed to be a fine man. The people generally are a verry social people and hospitable, and you may believe that the vegetables had to suffer while we stoped. The City is laid out in squares on a good plan. Streets wide. They irrigate the soil, haveing plenty of water from the Kenyons near by. Have raised this season some excellent wheat, and the valley for a hundred miles will be good tillage land. The people give one tenth of the products of their labor to the church for to feed the poor. They have not erected a temple as yet, but intend to soon as they have raised grain to keep them the while. While we have been here it has been verry warm in the Valley, but at a distance of sixteen miles the peaks of the Mountains are ever covered with snow. We did not visit the Lake some 20 miles distant, expecting to pass

---

President Young, mentioned below, was of course Brigham Young, who succeeded Joseph Smith as head of the Mormon Church in 1847, directed the mass migration of Mormons to Great Salt Lake Valley, and became first governor of the Territory of Utah (1849–1857).

³ The Staples Papers, C-D 158, Bancroft Library.

near it on our way. There is one place of interest that we frequently visited was a *warm sulpher* spring one mile above the city and reputedly healthy. It was uncomfortably warm on first entering but after a moment it was delightfull. Our men are much better in health and spirits than on entering the city. Quite a number had a bit of Mountain fever but are all well now. We started with high hopes of a speedy trip from here to our destination. We got started at four o'clock P.M., came out Eight miles to a junction of the road. Part of our men took the right [road] that hugged the mountains through the settlements. [*An insert, written upside down, at the bottom of the preceding page reads:* We passed a hot spring 4 m from the city. We could not bear a hand in it.] I together with the other part took the cut-off near the lake. We stoped at the first house and got supper and camped for the night. Distance 8 miles.

August 16

We went to one of the farm houses and got an excellent breakfast.

We then started out and went 10 miles farther and stopped by another farm house where we got dinner, which was very satisfactory to us.

Towards the close of the day the remainder of our party came in, they having taken another road which unites with this here. The country continues level as before and the soil very fertile. The Great Salt Lake is in full view, but in many places the sand plain, which is mixed with salt, looks like the lake at a distance, causing a very singular illusion.

[Staples]

This morning we packed up and started at 8 o'clock. Each man has two animals to take care of and pack, which makes the labor equel. This morning our road for several miles lay over a salt flat bottom, not a spear of grass. The ground moist with a salt crust on top. 15 miles brough us to the junction of the two roads. We camped in wait for the rest of the party to come up. They soon arrived and we all got dinner at a farm house. The farms all have to be irrigated to produce good crops. Here was a fine stream run near the house. This house unlike those in the city was made of logs. The "City houses were made mostly of douby bricks." Distance 15 miles.

August 17

We travelled as far as Weber River and encamped 1 mile beyond Capt. Browne's settlement,[4] which consists of several houses, the yard of which is surrounded by high palisades or wooden posts put uprightly in the ground and close together for protection against the Indians. Weber River is a beautiful clear stream, about 80 ft. in width, with cold, excellent drinking water and empties into the Great Salt Lake. I took a bucket and went to another small stream about 1 mile distant and just as I was dipping up some water, I heard a noise on the other side of the stream when I looked up and saw a Grizzly Bear just entering the stream above me, which he crossed over very quietly and struck into the woods beyond. He was about 6 or 8 feet in length and was rather a formidable looking fellow.

[Staples]

We moved on today and 17 miles brought us to the last house of the settlement. A mile beyond Capt. Brown's crossed Webber River and camped near another fork of the river two miles [beyond?]. Most of our men went back to Brown's to get dinner. I had a good bathe. After getting clean I met a man by the name of *Chase*[5] who lived on the

---

[4] Captain James Brown purchased Miles Goodyear's farm in behalf of the Mormon Church in 1847. The settlement was thereafter called Brown's Fort, or Brownsville, now part of Ogden, Utah.

[5] In 1848 Ezra Chase settled Mound Fort three miles north of Brown's Fort. This, too, is now a part of Ogden.

other side of the creek. I got permission to go home with him and get supper. On arriving at his house I found it the most agreeable family I had been in in the valley. A fine young lady presided at the table as mistress, mother being away. We had for supper *peas, corn, buiscuit, butter, milk, tea, coffey*— in fact all the heart of man could wish. After tea the old man went into the merits of the *Mormon* faith. After an evening's chat I retired to rest on a feather bed for the first time since leaving the States. Haveing been used to laying on the hard ground, my rest was not so pleasant as I antici- pated. The old man said he would provide a breakfast for the whole party.

August 18

We went to a farm house near by and got a most excel- lent breakfast, which was served in regular New England style by the ladies belonging to the family. As this is our last chance, there being no other house between this and Cal., we improved it right well. We travelled until we came to a clear, cold stream from the mountains, which we sup- posed was Box Elder Creek, and encamped. We saw a family of Indians, which I think were *Diggers*,[6] who had dried *service berries* and *carickets* mixed together, which serves them for food. They offered some to our folks, but they only accepted of the berries, which were quite good.

We still continue on the plain.

[Staples]

This morning I returned to camp and informed the *Boys* we could have breakfast and we geered up and went over at 9 o'clock, and a better breakfast we never sat too. This was our last hope till we get through.

After biding our *friends* goodby we moved on. Passed several springs of good water. We came to one after ten miles

[6] The Digger Indians belonged to the Shoshoni tribe. They were called Diggers because they depended in part on roots and seeds for their food.

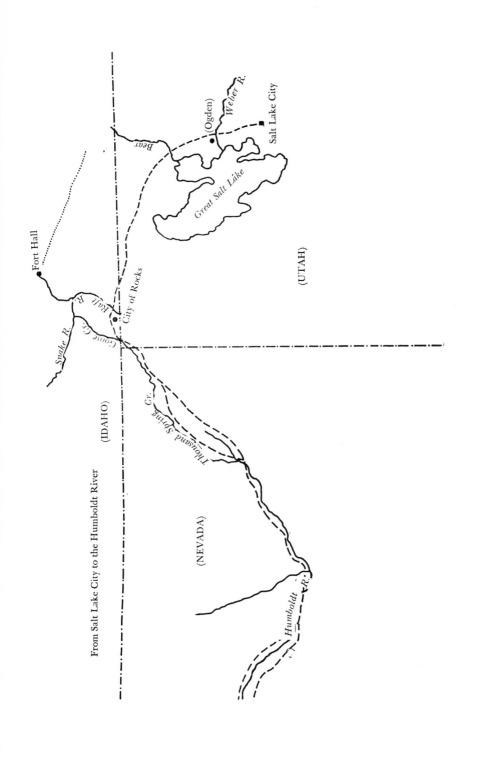

From Salt Lake City to the Humboldt River

and rushed down to quench our thirst, but found it so hot we could not bear our hand in it. Nearby was another cold, but salt. Great our disappointment. These springs are a wonder. We arrived at a small creek and camped for the night. Good grass and water. Distance 15 miles.

Sunday, August 19

6 miles brought us to Box Elder Creek, we having been mistaken in the Creek where we camped last night.

15 miles more, according to our guide book, we came to Bear River Crossing, but we believed the distance to be 20 miles. There has been a ferry established here all summer until the last week, when the waters have become so much fallen that it renders it useless. The river now is about 150 ft. wide, an average depth of 2½ feet. The waters are of a deep green, resembling sea water, but tastes fresh and sweet. The current is very swift and strong. We encamped on the opposite bank, where the feed is quite good, and it has been all the way from the City. The distance from the City is stated to be 75 miles by some of the guide books, others at 80.

[Staples]

Today we made a long drive. We passed several springs, some good, some warm and salt. Our road lay along the valley near the Bluffs. Some of them high and nearly perpendicular, forming numerous steeples and presenting some magnificent scenes. On our left we could see the Lake and marsh for miles, presenting the appearing of being covered with snow, the salt crust being verry white. We arrived at Bear River at 4 o'clock, Steep banks on either side, but with pack mules there is no difficulty in going down as up compared with out waggons. We camped after crossing on the banks of the river. Good grass here. One of our men shot several wild geese and ducks near our camp, which makes us a good meal. Distance 32 miles.

167

August 20

We now took a westerly course and after travelling about 25 miles through a suffocating dust and suffering severely from thirst we arrived at some warm salt springs, which notwithstanding their disagreeable taste, we drank very freely of. As there was no prospect of finding better water, we encamped here for the night. The grass, which consists of dry bunch grass, was quite plentiful and the animals recruited themselves very much upon this nutritious feed.

The salt water which we drank does not seem to quench our thirst much—its temperature is 80°.

[Staples]

Today we were off in good season. Three miles from camp we crossed a small stream of poor water called Malad Creek. Today our road passed along north of the Lake. Today about a west course. After leaving the creek, six miles brought us to a warm spring on the side hill. Here we filled our tanks, expecting to have a long drive to good water. We were not disappointed. The sun was hot in the extreme, the roads dusty—a kind of powder which would rise in clouds enough to suffacate a person. After twenty miles of such roads over some hills we came to a spring gushing out at a dozen places clear water. Men and animals rushed to it as if beside themselves, and what a disappointment! Just warm enough to be sickish and *salt*! Oh! horrors. We had traveled as far as the animals could bear and camp we must and make the best of it. We boiled some for coffee which only made it the *salter*. We have suffered as much today for want of water as any day since we started. Our men are all well, so we can stand it. Distance traveled today 29 miles.

August 21

After journeying about 15 miles we came to a beautiful spring. We all could have bowed down and worshiped, so refreshing were its precious waters to our parched and thirsty lips.[7] After enjoying its cooling waters for half an hour we started on again much refreshed and invigorated. 6 miles farther brought us to a small stream called Deep Creek. We followed on its banks a few miles and encamped. We are now in a large valley or plain surrounded upon all sides by hills and mountains. The soil consists of a mixture of sand and clay and is not very fertile, but our animals found a sufficient supply of bunch grass.

[Staples]

Today we started with our throats dry and husky, drinking so much warm salt water in hopes to find some good cold water. We traveled four hours over a mountainous country, and thank fortune we came to a spring in the mountains—cold pure water. This we considered a perfect *God Send.* Here we refreshed ourselves and animals for an hour, and moved on to a creek of *good* water—deep but narrow. We passed down the creek five miles and camped. Good grass. Here we found letters, papers, and sermons of an *Episcopal Clergyman* by name of Yeager who formerly preached in Boston. The writings of many hours scattered to the wind. We supposed he had died back on the road. His journal we found kept up to the South Pass. The last of it showed rather a depressed spirit. Poor fellow, he like many who started to improve their helth on this trip have found a grave on these plains. We met today a party returning to the city of Mormons. We could not learn much about them but supposed they were a party of *gold* diggers, as learned they expected some home soon. Distance traveled today 28 miles.

August 22

9 miles across a sandy plain brought us to a spring of pretty good water. 7 miles farther we came to the foot of a

---

[7] The spring is located on the Ward Ranch, about five miles east of the present town of Snowville, Utah.

mountain where there was a spring but it was impregnated with salt. We here took a northwesterly course and followed along the foot of the mountain until sundown when we struck into a ravine in the side of the mountain and encamped. The grass was excellent and there being a good spring close by and a good supply of wood made us quite at home.

Mr. Crist having gone back to find a mule that was left behind did not get into camp tonight. We obtained the best view of the Salt Lake that we have yet had when we first struck the mountain. There are several patches of snow upon the north side of the mountain.

[Staples]

This morning our road for twelve miles was across a plain covered with stunted sage and not a spear of grass. We came to a small spring of good water. Seven miles farther brought us to a mountain covered with stunted cedars. Here we found a weak spring, hardly furnishing water for ourselves and animals. We halted an hour or so. While here Brother Fred was attacked with a violent pain in his back. He was better in an hour and moved on with the train. We traveled till dark and came to a good spring. Here we camped, takeing our mules to a canyon near by for grass. Distance 26 miles.[8]

August 23

We left camp at 7, all in good spirits. Mr. Crist not having returned, we went on without him. We passed several springs and one clear, cool stream right from the snows of the mountains.

We stopped at noon upon the Carus [Cassia] Creek,[9] a

[8] On August 22, at Upper Newton Falls, David Staples' wife, Mary, gave birth to a baby girl, Mary Elizabeth.

[9] I have found seven spellings of the name of this tributary of Raft Creek in as many contemporaneous accounts. Staples spells it *Clajux. Cassia* is correct.

pretty little creek about 12 ft. wide with deep banks. After passing up this creek 10 miles we camped for the night. The trail leaves the stream here and turns to the right through the mts. Mr. Crist came into camp tonight, he having found the stray mule.

We found the Messrs. Rohrer Company waiting for us, they having started out from the City 3 or 4 days before we did and travelled slowly for us to overtake them.

[Staples]

This forenoon our road was some hilly till we struck the *Clajux Creek,* a distance of fourteen miles, passing several good springs.

This creek is four feet wide and two ft deep. Good water. We passed up the creek nine miles to where the road leaves it and camped. Here we found our friends Rohrer's & co who have traveled with us since leaveing Ft Kearny. They started from the city two days before we did and were in waiting for us. Grass poor. Distance 21 miles.

August 24

There has been quite a shower this morning, which laid the dust and made it quite comfortable travelling. 5 miles brought us to Ft. Hall road. The road after a few miles became very hilly and mountainous the rest of the day. Some of the views are very rich and beautiful, the distance, as far as the eye could reach being a succession of mts. rising one above another.

We struck Goose Creek and after travelling a few miles we encamped for the night.

The grass is fed pretty close, but our animals make out pretty well.

A great many of the rocks exhibit culcanous appearances.

[Staples]

Last night it rained quite hard most all night and this morning the clouds look lowery enough as they come over the mts. We packed up. Soon after, we struck over the ridge and had quite a shower.

It soon cleared off and the dust being laid we had the pleasantest time to travel that we have had for some time. Six miles brought us to the old road that passes *Ft. Hall* near Steeple Rock.[10] This is two elevations of rock rising from one base four or five hundred feet. After striking this road we had sixteen miles verry mountainous. Some verry steep decents where men hitch a tree behind waggons to hold back. This distance brought us to Goose Creek. We passed up three miles and camped for the night near the creek. Distance 25 miles.

August 25

It was found that one of our mules and 1 of Messrs. Rohrer's had been stolen during the night. Our men were immediately sent in all directions in search for them. Some of them soon struck the tracks of the delinquents, which led directly over the hills and mountains for about 10 miles, when they found themselves so closely pressed that they were obliged to leave them behind and escape as fast as they could and the men returned with Mr. Rohrer's mule and a horse belonging to a company that was encamped above us, but our mule could not be found.

[Staples]

This morning at daylight two of our mules was missing. One belonged to Rhorer, the other ours. We were soon up and a dozen horsemen looking for a track. They soon struck the trail in a Kenyon near by and a half a dozen followed in

---

[10] This is the City of Rocks—in 1849 also referred to as Steeple Rocks or Castle Rocks—an area comprising some twenty-five acres of rocks. Gould does not mention the area by name. Perhaps his map was not handy. Many articles that previously had been carried in the pockets that lined the canvas covers of the wagons now had to be carried in packs, and were not accessible until the packs were unrolled at night.

hot haste. After following the trail for ten miles through ravines and over steep mountains, they sude[n]ly came on one of the mules and a horse hitched. No men to be found. One man that was behind saw two men run down the opposite side of the hill in a ravine. He followed but lost sight of them. The party returned, bringing the horse and mule back. The horse we learned soon after was stolen four miles above from a small party. The mule found was Rohrer's. The probability is that a third man took some other course with ours, and we did not find it. We laid by for the day, giving the men a chance to attend to personal matters.

Sunday, August 26

We followed the creek until noon when we stopped 1 or 2 hours and rested our animals. We started on again and travelled until 10½. The moon shone very pleasantly and the evening being cool made it very agreeable travelling. It is supposed that we have made about 35 miles today; all excepting 4 or 5 miles I travelled on foot.

[Staples]

This morning our road was on the banks of the creek for twenty miles. Here we passed several ox teams who were recruiting. We halted at noon near the creek where the road leaves it, and then moved on sixteen miles to Hot Spring Valley. Arrived at 9 o'clock P.M. Near where we camped was a warm spring but became cold after running a few rods. The water was sweet and pure. No grass of any amount.

This has been a hard drive for our mules. 36 miles on poor feed.

August 27

Our encampment of last night was just on the edge of a valley known as "Thousand Spring Valley." We travelled all day in this valley, passing many excellent springs. The soil consists of a clayey, sandy formation, the wild sage, grease

173

wood, &c. being the chief growth. We encamped on a creek, the feed consisting of a coarse poor grass which is not very nutritious for our animals.

[Staples]

Today we have made a short drive. Passed down the valley over some few hills, passing several of the finest springs we have ever seen. This is called the Thousand Spring Valley. We came to a creek after traveling 15 miles with pools of water occasionally. We followed it five miles and camped. Poor grass and few willows to cook with. Distance traveled today 20 miles.

August 28

We followed along the same valley the greater part of the day and struck into a ravine which makes a passage through the mountains for the road.

We drove our animals about 1 mile from camp into a ravine where the grass was excellent. It being my watch, I went up with the rest of the watch and staid all night. I watched the first part of the night and slept the last part.

We were obliged to leave one of our horses behind that we traded for at the City [Salt Lake]. It was supposed that he had eaten some poisonous plant which made him sick.[11]

[Staples]

This morning we found that the grass our animals have had for a few days was not sufficient to sustain them on such long drives. Several of our horses laging yesterday. We packed up determined to stop [at] the first grass. After driving three miles we came to a bottom of blue grass, quite green. We halted four hours to give our mules time to fill up. After dinner we moved down the valley twelve miles to the mouth of Kenyon. One of our horses gave out and we

---

[11] The poisonous death camass grass is found in several western states, notably Colorado and Nevada.

left him. My horse we could not get into camp without great urging. The conclusion is the grass they have eaten has hurt them and [they] have had but little of that. Here there was no grass and we were compeled to drive our mules a mile up a ravine near by. For several nights back it has been verry cold. On the 25th water froze near our camp fire an inch thick, and this morning was equally cold. Distance 12 miles.

August 29

Our route continued in a southerly direction over a barren, wild sage country, the dust being very disagreeable. We encamped after turning to the right between the mountains. We were obliged to leave the horse which Mr. [Jesse] Winslow rode as far as the City in consequence of his becoming so weak and emaciated.

[Staples]

This morning our road lay over quite a ridge, and passing down a valley several miles we saw a spring on the right up on a side hill and halted for noon. After an hour's halt we moved on Some eight miles into a fine valley. Good grass and a fine spring. Here we camped for the night. The country over which we have passed for some days back has presented some high Mts on the right and left. Peaks covered with snow which makes our nights cold. The greatest inconvenience we suffer in traveling here is the dust. [It] is of a powdery character and traveling along will rise in clouds that will almost suffocate us. Roads besides are generally good for waggons. We find that packing saves much hard work climbing up hills and locking down. Distance today 25 miles.

August 30

We left the 3rd horse on the camp ground this morning which, together with the mule which we lost, has made quite a reduction in our animals. The soil is still barren and sandy

175

and the dust exceedingly disagreeable. We reached the Humboldt just at sunset and encamped.

The river is about 12 ft. wide here, the waters having the same color and taste as the Platte.

[Staples]

Today we have had a verry level road. After two hours travel we struck a fine creek which soon lost itselfe in the valley. At noon we came to a fine creek suposed to be the headwaters of the *Humbolt* River. Here we made our noon halt. This forenoon we left two of our horses, they haveing given out. After noon we made our drive down the river some 15 miles. Towards evening we lost our *frying* pans. This seemed our all as we gave up our *dutch ovens* at the city. We camped near the river after dark. We saw three Indians [who] appeared friendly. Here we herd of several head of cattle being stolen and several wounded with arrows. Here we found good grass. Distance 25 miles.

August 31

We travelled down to the Humboldt today and encamped upon its banks at night.

This is a very pleasant valley, bounded on each side by Mts. and hills of moderate height. The trail is very dusty, clouds of dust rising around the trains as they pass along, almost suffocating the traveller and animals. The stream is bordered by small willows which supplies the traveler with fuel. The grass is pretty good.

[Staples]

This morning four of us went back to look for our pans. After going back 5 miles we saw two men coming with them, they haveing found them half mile back. At M we packed up and moved on, crossing quite a stream towards night. Did not know the name. We saw a notice from *Mass* train stateing that an Indian had been shot and *Mortally wounded* and probably his tribe would be revenged. Five miles further we camped. Poor grass. Distance 15 miles. We have passed a large number of ox trains in the last few days, and the roads have been quite rough and dust beyond account, as fine as flour, rising in clouds. No wind during the day. The country has exhibited nearly the same appearance as has been seen over the first ridge.

September 1

We continued down the river and encamped at a bend in the river where the road divides, one following the river and the other passing over the hill, apparently making quite a cut off. The river widens as we follow it down, but the amount of water does not increase very fast. The grass is miserable.

[Staples]

Today our road lay along the river most of the time, occasionally leaveing it for a few miles. *Dust! Dust!! Dust!!!* Towards night we left it. Struck into a Kenyon and overe hills instead of keeping the river and camped near a small spring at 9 P.M. No feed passed a mile back from camp. We passed a Mormon train from Cal. They report Gold! Gold! Provisions reasonable. Fortunes made but 40 times as many spent. Society not yet under Uncle Sam's laws.

With this entry of September first, written in pencil, David Staples' journal comes to an end.

CHAPTER 11

To Sutter's Fort

The final phase of the journey to the Land of Gold began with a twelve-day trek along the Humboldt River, through seemingly endless sage-covered hills and rounded mounds rising in monotonous succession, one after the other. Although the Humboldt flowed through an arid region, there were green willows and occasional grassy patches along its banks.

Charles Gould's account resumes on the second day of their journey along the Humboldt.

Sunday, September 2

We took the road over the hill, thinking it would save considerable, but we found after travelling 15 miles that we had lost 4 or 5 miles by going the fartherest way.

We nooned on the banks of the river, the grass being quite good.

About 5 miles farther the road leaves the river to avoid a *cañon* and passes over the hills and mts. 20 miles before it strikes the river again. Night overtook us in the mts. and we were obliged to encamp for the night, but we were so fortunate as to find a spring and some grass for our animals.

September 3

We followed along through the mountains 10 miles farther, when the trail strikes the river again. We encamped for the night on the river bank again, the grass being quite good. Mr. Osborne found that one of his mules was missing and returned back for it and did not get into camp tonight. There was a Mormon train returning from California encamped near us last night. 2 of our men visited them and obtained some information from them respecting our road.

We hear a great many reports respecting Indians' depredations which have a sufficient foundation to make them regarded.

September 4

We travelled until noon and then encamped to wait for Mr. Osborne, much anxiety being felt in his behalf, it being feared that he may have fallen into the hands of some of the bands of strolling Indians who have committed so many depredations of late.

Much to our joy, he returned a[t] 4 P.M., he having been obliged to return back to the camp ground in the mts. to find his mule, which explained the cause of his absence.[1]

September 5

I came upon the watch last night, the moon shining beautiful and clear, making a splendid night.

We were off at sunrise and making a most excellent drive. We encamped upon the left bank of the river, where the grass was excellent. We met a train from Oregon bound for Ft. Hall with supplies. They had taken a southern route which strikes this road this side of the sink.[2]

We passed 56 wagons within 4 miles of camp tonight; all excepting the 10 from Oregon were bound to California.

---

[1] At dawn on September 4, Dr. Locke volunteered to go in search of the missing man. He had begun to fear the worst when far ahead he saw a lone rider. To his great relief it was Osborne, who hailed him from a small rise in the road. Dr. Locke related this incident to his children.

[2] In 1846 Jesse Applegate, who had crossed the plains to Oregon in 1843, explored the Humboldt Trail with several companions to establish a southern route to Oregon that would bypass Fort Hall.

September 6

The sound of the bugle's sweet notes aroused us from our slumbers before the sun had risen, and breakfast was eaten and we were on our way at 6.

We took the left bank of the river, the old trail going to the right, which saves us about 5 miles travel and the dust was not so heavy.

The soil in many places is strongly impregnated with *saleratus,* which rises up with the dust, causing much distress to the animals.

4 Antelopes were seen this morn. We made our drive without stopping at noon and camped upon the left bank of the river.

September 7

We were off in good season again this morning and followed along the left bank of the river the whole day.

The general appearance of the country has the same monotonous look as it has already borne for the last 150 miles. Wild sage, grease wood &c. border the bottom which today has a pretty good growth of grass, and after 20 miles from our last night encampment was a very heavy growth of grass. Many teams are recruiting here, preparatory to crossing the desert. We encamped on a splendid spot of grass.

September 8

We have concluded to stop and recruit today.

The men are engaged in washing and mending their clothes and doing such little jobs as the journey has rendered necessary.

Dr. Haines and Mr. [Calvin] Fifield arrived in camp tonight, they being sent on by the Granite State Company to make arrangements for them previous to their arrival in Cal. There is another gentleman with them.[3]

[3] This was J. P. Hoyt, also of the Granite State Company. Hoyt and Fifield later opened a sign and paint shop in Sacramento.

September 9

We have made about 28 miles today, but had the misfortune to find none but poor grass for our animals.

The wind has blown very strong, causing the heavy dust to penetrate every thing. Altogether it has been the most disagreeable day that we have yet travelled. The southern Oregon road leaves this 2 miles above our encampment.

September 10

We followed the river, occasionally passing over a point of the bluffs which some times extend so near the river as to leave no room for the road between them and the river.

We again had the bad luck to find a poor camping ground, the grass for miles being eaten closely to the ground.

The road which we passed last night and supposed to be the Oregon road proved to be a cut off which would have saved us 6 miles if we had known of it. The true Oregon road leaves about ½ of a miles from this encampment.

September 11

After following the river for a few miles, the road strikes across a sand plain for about 20 miles when it passes through a crooked ravine and strikes the river again. The sand bluffs have closed the river in, barely giving it room for the whole day, but here it spreads out in the form of being a circular basin and is covered with a growth of willows. Night overtaking us here, we were obliged to stop here, forbidding as [the] place was, there being no other place near.

Sunday, September 12

We travelled 10 or 12 miles and then turning 2 or 3 miles to the left of the road we found a beautiful camping ground of most luxuriant grass surrounded by the sand bluffs. We have determined to stop here and recruit preparatory to crossing the desert. We cut some hay to help our animals after leaving the sink.

This oasis in the desert, known as the Great Meadows, lay adjacent to the grayish-white Humboldt Sink, which extended eastward as far as the eye could see. Although travelers in 1849 had heard descriptions of the Great Meadows—it was known as excellent place to rest and recruit and was even noted on maps—until they actually saw it few could believe that it would be so large and luxuriant. During their stop here the Boston-Newton party sold their remaining horses, and depended on their mules for the rest of the journey.[4] Using sheath knives, they cut some of the tall, green grass to carry with them, rolling it into fifteen-pound bundles. Here also, they took time to trim their hair and beards—outdoor barber shops were a common sight along the trail—and to attend to such chores as washing clothes and mending canvas covers.[5]

A forty-niner who reached the Great Meadows four weeks earlier than the Boston-Newton men wrote this description of the scene in his journal:

> This marsh for three miles is certainly the liveliest place that one could witness in a lifetime. There is some two hundred and fifty wagons here all the time. Trains going out & others coming in & taking their places is the constant order of the day. Cattle & mules by the hundreds are surrounding us, in grass to their knees, all discoursing sweet music with the grinding of their jaws. Men too are seen hurrying in many different ways & everybody attending to his own business. Some mowing, some reaping, some carrying, some packing the grass, others spreading it out to dry, or collecting that already dry & fixing it for transportation. In fact the joyous laugh & the familiar sound of the whetted

[4] The article in the Newton *Graphic*, November 27, 1896, based on the Benjamin Burt letters, after referring to the shortage of grass, remarks that "mules could get along with very little food. For this reason [the party] sold their horses before crossing the great 60 mile desert beyond Salt Lake City."

[5] The Staples Papers, C-D 158, Bancroft Library.

scythe gives an air of happiness & content around that must carry the wearied travellers through to the "Promised Land." The scene reminds one much of a large encampment of the army, divided off into separate & distinct parties, everybody minding his own business and letting other people alone.[6]

At Great Meadows there was a choice of two routes into California. One took a westward course over barren desert hills to the Truckee River and the Donner Pass of ill-fated memory;[7] the other, which the Boston-Newton company elected to follow, ran southwest to Carson Pass over the Carson Sink.

A curious incident occurred as they were preparing to leave the Great Meadows and start across the Sink of the Humboldt. Charles Gould does not report it, but David Staples wrote of it some years later.

> Just as we were packing up to leave while the sun was about half an hour high, on looking across the meadows we saw a stalwart fellow stalking toward us and in the rays of the setting sun he seemed about seven or eight feet high. He had on a white fur or silk hat, with a red string tied about the middle of it, from the brim to the crown, and not another rag of any kind. He walked like a monarch and striding into camp, he asked for bread and we told him we could not get any for him, it was all packed up. He then asked for whiskey, and we told him we had not any in camp, as we had not. The Indian looked at us for a moment rather

---

[6] Quoted from David Morris Potter, ed., *Trail to California; The Overland Journal of Vincent Geiger and Wakeman Bryarly* (New Haven: Yale University Press, 1945), p. 184–185. The entry for August 9 was written by Bryarly.

[7] In 1846 a party from Illinois organized by Jacob and George Donner were snowbound in the High Sierras. In the end only forty-five of the eighty-nine men and women who left Fort Bridger reached their destination, and they had practiced cannibalism to survive. The misinformation in Lansford W. Hastings' popular *Emigrants' Guide to Oregon and California* (1845) was in part responsible for their tragic experience.

scornfully, and said, "White man lie, God damn," and turned on his heel and stalked off across the prairie.[8]

Crossing the Sink of the Humboldt took two days, as Charles Gould relates.

September 13

We moved on about 16 miles and encamped again to give the animals farther time to recruit.

The waters have ceased to flow, the surplus being absorbed by the soil, causing what is called the *slough* but I think should more properly be called the *sink*.

The grass covers several hundred acres with an excellent rich growth, enough to supply all the emigration that will ever be likely to pass this way. There are a great many trains here cutting grass to carry them across the desert.

September 14

We moved 6 miles this morning to the end of the sink and stayed until 5, when we started on our dreaded journey across the desert.

After a few miles we struck on to a large, perfectly level plain, completely destitute of all vegetation. We travelled on until 10 P.M. when we encamped near the *sink* and after giving out a little hay to our animals, we retired to bed in this lonely, desolate region.

We came across a small company which had taken the wrong road[9] which led them away from the slough and did not give them an opportunity to take in a supply of water and consequently they were suffering severely from thirst. I gave an old man a drink from my canteen which seemed to have done him more good than a purse of *gold*.

---

[8] Statement of D. J. Staples, 1878, in the Staples Papers, C-D 158, Bancroft Library.

[9] At this point the old trail led directly west to the mountains, and there was no sign at the cutoff to the Great Meadows.

September 15

We were off again at sunrise, this place having no attractions for us. We saw several pools or springs of stagnant water covered over with a greenish slime and are said to be very strongly impregnated with alkali. There were several wells dug near our camp, about 4 feet deep, but the water was so strong of sulphur that our animals would not taste of it.

3 miles from the sink the road leaves the old road which passes by the hot *springs* and goes to the left. In a few miles we came to an alkali spring around which were several dead oxen.

We soon entered upon a large level plain several miles in diameter being entirely destitute of all vegetation and having the appearance of a field just sown with grain and rolled down smooth. The *mirage* was here seen in great perfection and beauty, presenting a large and beautiful lake of clear water, on the surface of which was reflected the shrubs and objects on the shore. We stopped at noon where some one had dug a well, but the water was so salt that neither our men or animals would drink it. We fed out the remainder of our hay to our animals, and taking a dinner ourselves we started on again. We have passed more than 100 dead oxen today and a great many deserted wagons. We struck Carson River at 10 after the hardest day's work that we have ever performed.

We left 2 mules behind which have got exhausted. The rest looked much better than we expected.

September 16

We started off before breakfast this morning and went about 6 miles up the river and camped for the day to rest ourselves and animals.

This stream is about 50 ft. wide and 1 ft. deep. The

water is clear and delicious, we knowing well how to appreciate it after being obliged to use the water that we have of late.

Some tall Cotton Wood trees were scattered along the banks of the stream, which make a very agreeable sight to us as we have seen no trees of large size for several hundred miles. We are encamped under some noble old trees whose limbs afford us a most acceptable shade. This river sinks in the desert a few miles below where we struck it; it rises in the *Sierra Nevada.*

September 17

We travelled a few miles upon the river bottom and struck across a barren country covered with wild sage and grease wood to cut off a bend in the river about 12 miles, when we struck the river again and followed it up 2 miles & encamped in a valley well supplied with rich grass.

The Messrs. Rohrer and company moved on and left us as they did not wish to delay any longer. We are encamped in a beautifuul grove of large Cotton Wood trees.

There are many complaints made of the Indians shooting their arrows into the emigrants' oxen and wounding them, thus obliging them to leave them behind.

September 18

There are 2 roads here, one of which follows the river and the other makes a *cut off*, in consequence of the river making a bend. We took the *cut off* which leads across a barren sand plain destitute of all vegetation except wild sage &c.

The trail has been generally hard and smooth and very straight. We struck the river again in 20 miles from where we left it, making a saving of about 10 miles. We then passed about 6 miles farther up the river and encamped. The Rohrers took the river road and passed us after we were encamped and camped about 4 miles above us. The *mirage* was seen in great beauty today as we passed over a perfectly level plain.

187

Sunday, September 19

We were under way in excellent season this morning, all being in good spirits and prepared for a hard day's work. After following the river 6 miles farther up, we left the river again and went 12 miles over a very stony and rough road, when we struck the river again and followed it up into a most beautiful valley about 15 miles farther and encamped, very much tired out.

We are now in the *Sierra Nevada* mts., some of the ranges being very lofty. They are on fire in many places, which are probably the work of Indians.

September 20

We continued up this beautiful valley [Hope Valley] about 22 miles and stopped for the day. This valley is 12 or 15 miles in width in the middle and 42 long. It is covered with a most luxuriant growth of grass, enough to feed thousands of cattle. Along the borders, next to the mts., are a great many streams of pure cold water running into the valley. We also passed some *hot springs,* some being *hotter* than a person could hold his hands in.

The sides of the mountains are covered with tall, straight, handsome Norway Pines.

September 21

After travelling 4 miles farther we came to the end of the valley and turning to the right, we entered a narrow *ravine,* bordered on both sides by perpendicular and very high granite rocks. A branch of Carson [West Carson] River passes through this *Gorge.*[10]

The road is very rocky, making it very dangerous for wagons, many of which lie by the sides of the road broken to pieces.

The distance through the ravine is 4 miles. We passed springs of pure cold water every few rods. After leaving this,

[10] Grover Hot Springs State Park now marks this gorge.

From the Humboldt to Sutter's Fort

the road turns in a southerly direction 5 miles, when we reach the foot of the first mountain. There is a pretty lake here called *Red* Lake.[11] Now came the hard labor which we have so long been dreading, and it seemed almost impossible to ever rise the mountain, but we must, so we set ourselves at work, clambering up the steep sides of the mt., and after a great deal of hard climbing we succeeded in reaching the summit, but the task was almost too much for some of our mules, which have got very much reduced by the journey. It is 1 mile from the foot to the top and very rocky at that. We passed 3 or 4 miles down the other side and camped, very much tired out.

September 22

We came to a small valley in the centre of which was a lake [Blue Lake] making one of the most beautiful views which I have ever beheld as I looked down upon it from our elevated situation. We then passed through the valley and struck the foot of the Main Mt. We rose this mountain by a gradual ascent, which is five miles to the summit,[12] which we reached at 11—a feat we congratulated ourselves upon very much. We found several banks of snow and had some sport *snowballing* each other. We melted some snow in our dippers and gave 3 cheers and drank it. The view from the summit was grand beyond description. We then travelled 15 miles amongst the smaller mountains, descending a great deal, and encamped.

September 23

We remain encamped today to recruit our animals which

[11] At certain times of the day the red stone mountain casts a shadow on the water giving it a reddish appearance, hence the name of the lake.

[12] California Highway 88 passes over part of this route. At the summit of the road a marker gives the elevation as 8,753 feet. Embedded in the marker is a piece of wood bearing the name of Kit Carson. The wood came from a tree that stood a thousand feet above the present highway on the summit of the trail traversed by the forty-niners.

have got reduced pretty low from the severe labor of crossing the mountains.

My watch came on last night and as we were surrounded by fallen timber which was very dry, we set fire to them to make the animals visible. They burned with remarkable brilliancy, rendering very animal in the *corral* visible.

Some of the men who went out hunting brought in 2 fine Deer which made quite an agreeable luxury to us as we had not tasted fresh meat for some time.

We are all of us in fine spirits as we look back upon what we have passed over and think of the hardships and toils that we have gone through.

September 24

We resumed our journey again this morning in good season. The road has followed along the tops of a high ridge almost the whole day, gradually descending as we pass on. The dust has been exceedingly disagreeable today, it being 6 and 8 in. deep, and rising in clouds around us as we travelled along. We have passed many noble and beautiful pines, some of them measuring from 7 to 10 ft. in diameter and upwards of 200 ft. in height, many of them rising 60 ft. without a limb, holding their proportions and size remarkably well.

After a long day's drive we encamped in a hollow without any feed for our animals.

September 25

We continued on our journey in hopes soon of being out of the woods. Our route was about the same as yesterday until noon, when we entered a pleasant valley which seemed truly pleasant to us after the rough scene that we have left.[13]

13 Gould is probably referring to Grizzly Flats. Its terrain was composed mostly of rocks, broken here and there by scrub pines, the only vegetation among the jumbled heap of stone. The Boston-Newton company then entered what came to be called Pleasant Valley. A few oaks are still standing there.

We found some people here engaged in *prospecting* or seeking for gold.

We continued on until night when we encamped where there were many people engaged in searching for gold—how successful they were we could not ascertain. We were obliged to fall some Oak trees to browse our animals upon who look very gaunt & hungry.

Sunday, September 26

We did not travel but half a day in consequence of stopping to feed our animals upon some grass that we were so fortunate as to find for them. The valley is covered with beautiful groves of Oak whose symmetrical forms rise all around us.

We are continually meeting teams bound for the mines—which lie mostly to the right of us. The principal places are called Weaver Town, situated on Weaver Creek, and Mormon Island.

On the morning of September 26, the company used up the last of their flour and bacon. Hangtown (Placerville) was ten miles to the north of their route. It was the Sabbath, and a vote was taken to determine if they should go into the village for a square meal or continue on the trail until they came to good forage. The mules had gone two days without nourishing feed, and this was the first occasion in their journey that there was a chance the men might go hungry. The majority voted to continue on the trail.[14]

At noon, tall, wide-spreading oaks and green grass came into view; and, as they drew near the spot, the travelers found a spring.[15] This was the last campsite of the Boston-Newton party on their journey across the continent.

[14] The Staples Papers, C-D 158, Bancroft Library.

[15] The town of Shingle Springs is now at this last campsite. In 1950, a stone marker was placed there and dedicated. The State of California pro-

September 27

We started with the intention of reaching Sutters tonight, which we accomplished by nine P.M., both men and animals being very much fatigued.

We passed several *Ranches* or farming establishments and a great many drinking shops. We made about 40 miles today. Hurrah for California! Here we are all safe, and we don't care whether school keeps or not.

---

vided a large bronze plaque and the blueprint for the marker, which was paid for by descendants of the men who made up the Boston-Newton company. They also gave a second marker, listing the names of members of the company.

CHAPTER 12

The Disbanding of the Company

Charles Gould's diary ends with the jubilant entry of September 27, and the following account of the four weeks before the company disbanded is necessarily based in part on conjecture. I have tried to indicate the documentary sources of my account. In addition, there are statements in letters and in accounts written years after the events described, but they were not completely accurate. What happened to Jesse Winslow's records as treasurer of the company and to the notes of the secretary, S. D. Osborn, is still a mystery.

A good description of Sutter's Fort, as it appeared in June, 1846, standing alone "in solitary state, on an eminence commanding the approaches on all sides," was written by Lieutenant Warren Joseph Revere:

> The fort consists of a parallelogram enclosed by adobe walls, eighteen feet high and a yard thick, with bastions at the angles. The walls of these towers are four feet thick and their embrasures are so arranged as to flank the terrain on all sides. . . . A good house sits in the center of the area, serving as officer's quarters, armory, guard and state rooms; also for a kind of interior citadel. There is a second wall on the inner face, the space between it and the outer wall being

193

roofed and divided into workshops, quarters, etc. The usual offices are present; also a well of good water.

Corrals for the cattle and horses of the garrison are conveniently placed where they are under the eye of a guard. Cannon frown—an inveterate habit of cannon—from the various embrasures. The ensemble presents the dreamer's ideal of a romantic border fortress. It must have astonished the natives as their hands, guided by the white man's skill, made the white walls rise out of the lovely virgin plain.[1]

Lieutenant Revere's description of the exterior of the fort still applied in 1849. By this time, however, Captain Sutter was living in his new home some miles away, and the two-story central building, described above, "was occupied by Rufus Hitchcock, the upper story being used as a boarding house. The bar was kept open night and day."[2] The buildings along the walls inside the compound were used as shops for merchandise, and one was a blacksmith shop. Although Sutter's Fort is now within the city limits of Sacramento, in 1849 the few houses that marked the beginning of the future city were about a mile away.

It was fairly late on the evening of September 27 that the Boston-Newton party reached the fabulous fort, "both the men and the animals being fatigued," as Charles Gould wrote. By the time they had pitched their tents and tethered the mules it was about ten o'clock, and some of the men went to bed with no supper while others went out in search of a place to eat.

The next morning the mail was picked up at the fort and distributed.[3] It requires no wild stretch of the imagination to picture the eagerness with which the men opened their letters and

---

[1] Quoted in Julian Dana, *Sutter of California* (New York: Press of the Pioneers, 1934), p. 231.

[2] *History of Sacramento County* (Oakland: Thompson and West, 1880), p. 46.

[3] It will be remembered that George Winslow had written to his wife, "Direct your letters to Sutters Fort."

how hungrily they devoured the news. Now David Staples learned that he had a daughter and Charles Gould that he had a son. To Dr. Locke came the distressing word that his younger brother, Elmer, had been accidentally shot and was in serious condition at Mokelumne Hill. The news was doubly shocking, since the doctor did not even know that his brother, succumbing to the gold fever, had started west via Panama after the Boston-Newton party left Independence.

Before noon, Dr. Locke set out for Mokelumne Hill, a distance of about fifty miles southeast of Sacramento. When the discovery of gold became widely known, Mokelumne Hill had been one of the first of the mining towns to spring up. It was founded in 1848 by veterans of the Mexican War, former members of the Stevenson Regiment of New York. By September 1, 1849, the village consisted mostly of shacks built on top of the high hill and of tents which were pitched on the slope stretching down to the river where miners staked out claims. When Dr. Locke arrived at the river crossing, his doctor's satchel on the side of his pack, the news soon spread that a physician was in camp. Before he had time to ask questions, a man rushed out of a tent and begged the doctor to stop and see a very sick man. When the doctor stepped into the tent he found, much to his surprise, that the patient was his brother.[4]

About two weeks after the doctor's departure from Sutter's Fort, word came that he was ill at Mokelumne Hill and that he needed help. Nathaniel Loring volunteered to go there and care for him.[5]

In the meanwhile matters had been going forward at the camp. Despite their eagerness to get out to the gold fields, the first thing to be done was to procure the goods which had been shipped from Boston to San Francisco aboard the *Helen Augusta*. David Staples, Benjamin Burt, and Albion Sweetzer were dele-

[4] Related to the author by Dr. Locke's children.
[5] Newton *Graphic*, November 27, 1896.

gated to go to San Francisco and arrange to have the goods transferred to a river boat, which would bring it up the Sacramento River.[6]

Evidently the men were able to travel by steamboat to San Francisco; two such vessels—the *Sacramento* and the *McKim*—were in service at that time.[7] However the men had some difficulty in arranging transport for their goods back from San Francisco. Both steamers apparently already had their full complement of freight, and the only craft available to them was a sailboat. It moved briskly enough out of the harbor at San Francisco, but on the Sacramento River it was another story. The boat had to fight its way up the long stream, and as it laid over at night the trip took two to three weeks.[8] Benjamin Burt said that he "suffered more in returning from San Francisco than at any time during the overland trip."[9]

When Dr. Locke returned to the Sutter's Fort camp, he brought with him the tragic news that Nathaniel Loring had contracted pneumonia at Mokelumne Hill and died within a few days. He had been buried at Mokelumne Hill Cemetery. When a last tribute was paid to Loring by his trail companions, Benjamin Burt recited a psalm and once again it fell to Albion Sweetzer to offer a prayer for the departed member of the group. The sad duty of informing Anne Loring of her husband's death was delegated to Burt.[10]

---

[6] Unless otherwise indicated, information given about the disbanding of the company is derived from the Staples Papers, C-D, 158 and C-D, 289.1, at the Bancroft Library.

[7] The *Sacramento* began service in July, 1849, and the *McKim* on September 20, 1849.

[8] According to an item in the *Alta*, January 4, 1850, quoted in *History of Sacramento County*: "Well do we remember the early days of inland transportation, the tedious days and sleepless nights (there were mosquitoes in those times) passed sailing up the Sacramento." The item refers to "the torments of those trips, two to three weeks duration."

[9] Newton *Graphic*, November 27, 1896.

[10] *Ibid.*

Although originally it had been the company's intention to work together, it now seemed that it would be better to operate independently. As David Staples later reported:

> We sent parties in different directions to see if we could work together to advantage, and the committees reported that it was better to dissolve, and so we sold our provisions and the utensils we had brought out right on the levee. Our goods brought fabulous prices. A cooking stove that cost sixty dollars in Boston we sold for four hundred, and everything in proportion, so we had plenty of funds.[11]

According to Albion Sweetzer, some of the goods were sold on the levee and the rest moved to where the state capitol now stands and there auctioned off. Unfortunately Sweetzer did not profit from the sale. On his return from the tiresome journey to San Francisco, he confided to one of the other members of the Boston-Newton company that he was worried about the low state of his finances. The man offered to buy Sweetzer's share in the company's merchandise for one hundred dollars—an offer which Sweetzer promptly accepted. He bitterly regretted his hasty decision when the goods brought in such a handsome sum, but he never did reveal the name of the man who had profited at his expense.[12]

The Boston-Newton Joint Stock Association formally disbanded on October 25, 1849. On that date Charles Gould wrote a letter to his father who recorded its contents in his journal on January 9, 1850, the day he received it.

> The letter was written at Sacramento City on the 25th of October last. Charles and his associates reached the city on

[11] The Staples Papers, C-D 158, Bancroft Library.

[12] For statements by Albion Sweetzer, see *History of Sacramento County*, p. 292, and *Illustrated History of Sacramento County* (Chicago: Lewis Publishing Co., 1890), pp. 566–567.

the 27th of September, having been 165 days from Boston and 133 days from Independence on the frontier of Missouri. In the letter he states that the company to which he belonged has broken up and scattered in different directions, for the reason that it was the experience of all companies that the digging of gold could not be carried on to advantage in large companies.

Thenceforward, each man of the company was on his own. Among the group who had made the journey across the continent a goodly number were destined to make their mark on the country. Some would not only find the proverbial pot of gold, but would go on to reap rewards beyond all expectation. Others would leave the Land of Gold, and go on to new ventures elsewhere. But whatever fortune awaited them in the years ahead, one and all would cherish the memory of the adventures they had shared on the overland trail to California in 1849.

EPILOGUE

Although the fortunes of the members of the Boston-Newton Joint Stock Association after its disbanding are outside the scope of this book, it will be of interest, I think, to include a brief glimpse of how they fared in later years, so far as I have been able to discover.

The information is presented in summary form, with the most attention given to those with whom we have become best acquainted in the diaries of Charles Gould and David Staples, including the diarists themselves. The sources from which this information has been derived are indicated in the Note on Sources.

After the entries on Gould and Staples, the members of the company are listed in alphabetical order.

CHARLES GOULD
Charles Gould's activities after the disbanding of the Boston-Newton company are reported in the journal kept by his father, Major Gould, back in Walpole, Massachusetts. On January 9, 1850, Major Gould received the first letter from Charles "written at Sacramento City on the 25th of October last." On February 7 he wrote:

> Another letter from Charles. It was written from the North Fork of the American River, five miles above the South Fork and thirty-four miles from Sacramento City. Charles writes that he is now associated with James Wilson, Walton Felch, and Albion Sweetzer of the old company, who

199

have built a log house at that place, which gives them good quarters for the rainy season, with a full supply of provisions for the winter. Charles says he has dug gold enough to supply himself with the necessities for the winter, and that he is in excellent health and spirits, and ready to begin digging as soon as the rain permits.

From the same source we learn that James Wilson left California in the autumn of 1849 for home, and on February 7, 1850, Major Gould called on him in Roxbury. Wilson set on the return trip to California on February 26, taking with him daguerreotypes of members of the Gould family for Charles. On March 12, Major Gould wrote:

> Charles sent home his first parcel of gold dust from California. It weighed ½ pound Troy weight making the parcel worth $105.39. Charles dug the gold in the month of January, although it rained about half of the month. The gold was brought by the Express of Adams and Company of Boston, at a charge of 8 percent, including insurance paid in advance.

On April 10, Major Gould received "another letter from Charles, also 8½ oz. of gold worth about $148."

The following fall Gould and Wilson explored the mining region farther north and west of their first claim, going up over the San Juan Ridge and on to Sears Diggings, later renamed St. Louis. They then went to Ophir City (Oroville) and finally settled down at Wyman Ravine in Butte County.

The months spent in mining gold had stimulated Gould's great desire to live in California. Accordingly, when the railroad bonds his father had purchased for him with the little pouches of gold dust made a neat stack, he was ready to bring his family to California. He began his journey to San Francisco on June 28, 1852, and embarked from there for Panama aboard the steamer *Golden Gate.* Crossing the Isthmus involved a journey of a day and a

200

half on muleback and a two-hour ride on the partially completed railroad. He then proceeded to Key West, Florida, aboard the *Eldorado* and from Key West to New York aboard the *Empire City.* There followed the train journey to Boston, and on July 27 Major Gould recorded in his journal:

> My son, Charles, arrived home from California. He has been absent three years and three months. His health is good, and his appearance as favorable as when he left here. On this occasion my children were all at home once more, which to me was an interesting meeting. Charles left the same day for the purpose of visiting his wife and two children at Hartland in the state of Maine.

Unfortunately, Gould was suffering from malaria; and though he made a good recovery, the fact that he had contracted the disease on his journey increased his difficulties when he tried to persuade his wife, Betsey, that the family should move west. In time he seemed to have succeeded and wrote his old partner, James Wilson, that he expected to arrive in San Francisco with his family about November 5, 1854. But as the date to start for California drew near, Betsey Gould's courage faltered. At this time Minnesota Territory was being boomed in New England papers, and the Goulds compromised on a farm in Minnesota. In the spring of 1855 Gould made an exploratory trip there, and on May 4 Major Gould reported the results in his journal.

> Received a letter from my son, Charles, in which he says, "I have found a place that suits me. It is located about half way up Lake Pepin, on the Minnesota side. Lake Pepin is an extention of the Mississippi river and is about two miles wide for nearly thirty miles, with nice clean water and gravelly shores. There is a valley on this side, running parallel with the river, some three miles wide by ten or twelve miles long, which I think is the most pleasant place I ever saw. I was so pleased with it that I was determined

to locate here if possible, and finding a claim of 160 acres, that was occupied, which suited me in every respect, I bought the man's claim to the land, and when the land is surveyed I shall pay the regular government price, $1.25 per acre. There is a small log house and one acre broken."

Betsey Gould and the two children made the trip west by stage, train, and steamboat, and on June 6 Major Gould recorded that he had learned of their safe arrival. By this time, Charles had added two rooms to the log cabin and had planted a garden.

Their third spring on the farm, in 1858, Minnesota became a state, and that year Charles Gould built a large frame house out of hardwood lumber cut from oaks on his farm. He had fine neighbors and friends, and was successful in his farming venture, but he could not forget California. Evidently, too, he had built up a great deal of interest in that faraway place among his friends, for in 1862 several families in the community planned to drive overland to California during the summer. Again he wrote to his trail and mining companion, James Wilson, and in his reply Wilson discussed "land to settle on," prices, routes, and the kind of livestock to bring.

But Charles Gould did not leave his farm in Minnesota, after all. It was destined to be his home for the rest of his life. On June 22, 1907, when he and Betsey celebrated their sixtieth wedding anniversary, he was still doing chores about the place: milking the cows, feeding the chickens, looking after the beautiful bay mare which he hitched to the buggy each day to drive into Lake City for the mail. He put on a pair of store spectacles to read the newspapers, but he showed no signs of advanced age except that it took somewhat longer to perform all the chores.

In 1911, after a visit from a representative of the Nebraska State Historical Society in connection with the George Winslow monument (see below), Charles Gould began to read his 1849 diary aloud. Betsey Gould recalled receiving his letters from Fort Kearny and Fort Laramie, and the long wait before the first letter posted from Sutter's Fort had reached her. They looked at the flowers pressed in the book—mayflowers picked while the party was in Missouri, prairie pinks from Kansas, wild roses from Nebraska, daisies from Wyoming—and other mementos of trail days. Gould arranged to have a typewritten copy of the dairy given to the Nebraska State Historical Society, and copies also were made for the Winslow and Lord families.

A year later, when Gould received the newspaper accounts of the dedication of the Winslow monument at Fairbury, Nebraska, on October 12, 1912, he and his daughter Rosa were alone in the big house. Betsey had died on January 8, 1912. On December 29, 1913, when he was close to ninety, Charles came to the end of his journey. He was survived by two sons and two daughters; a fifth child had died in infancy.

DAVID STAPLES

Following the disbanding of the Boston-Newton company, David and Fred Staples, Daniel Easterbrook, Milo Ayer, Robert Coffey, William Nichols, and George Thomason started out together for Kings River, south of Sacramento, but when they heard about the rich diggings at Winter's Bar on the Mokelumne River they decided to investigate the possibilities there instead. However, a brief look at mining operations convinced the Staples brothers that this occupation was not for them. They bought extra mules and pack saddles at Stockton and went into business hauling merchandise to the mines. The other five men began to mine at once in the Mokelumne Hill area, and during the following year they did well.

In February, 1850, with financial help from his companions, David Staples bought a tract of rich farming land which he described as "three leagues along the south bank of the Moke-lumne River by one league out in the uplands." The deed was filed in the name of David J. Staples and William H. Nichols, and the property was owned equally, although it always was known as the Staples Ranch. Ayer, Easterbrook, Coffey, Thomason, and Fred Staples used the ranch as their headquarters for several years, and Nichols remained there until it was sold in the early 1860's. Staples was surprised to learn that along with the land and chattels, he also had acquired a slave—a Mexican peon named Jesus. He was immediately given his freedom, but Jesus preferred the status quo—he wanted to go on cooking for his new owners just as he had done for his old ones as long as he could remember.

The first owner of this property was an Englishman, Tom Smith, who had received it as a gift from the Mexican government in 1844. John Laird had bought the grant in the early part of 1849, and had operated a ferry during the year that he owned the land. When Staples and his partners took over the property, they bought a good boat and continued to operate the ferry. By the spring of 1850 there was enough ferry business to warrant building a bridge. The crossing was on the road between Sacramento and San Jose, and since it was the only road connecting these two important points it was much traveled during the early years of the gold rush. Staples and Nichols financed and constructed the bridge at a cost of three thousand dollars. (They were unable to collect any toll from the first user of the new structure—a large grizzly bear.) Early that same spring the material for a two-story frame house arrived; it had been shipped from Maine around Cape Horn. The lumber was cut ready to assemble; windows and doors had been shipped with frames. Inasmuch as lumber was at a great premium, partitions were made by covering the two-by-fours that marked off the rooms with heavy muslin or canvas. Milo Ayer supervised the construction of the house, which was quite a novelty in California, where one-story ranch houses predominated.

A group of Wasook Indians inhabited land adjacent to the ferry on the north side of the river. There were one hundred and twenty of them when Staples and his partners took over the ranch. They were a friendly tribe and remained on good terms with the New Englanders, providing them with help on the ranch.

In August, 1850, David Staples began the journey back to Massachusetts, via Panama, to collect his family; and on November

26—Thanksgiving Day—he started on the return trip to California with his wife, Mary, and their little daughter, Mary Elizabeth. Accompanying them was Milo Ayer's wife, Phoebe, and their two-year-old daughter, Belle. Mary Staples described the party's arrival at the Staples Ranch on January 8, 1851:

> It was about three in the afternoon, getting a little cool and four miles further to go—through the most lovely natural park of live oak trees that can possibly be imagined; the road as level and firm as the best shell road. At last we reached the Staples Ranch. Suddenly, the road descended quite a cliff, showing its beautiful scenery. As we neared the house a group of Indians and their huts was the first thing that met our eyes. Their tule huts reminded us of the native houses on the Isthmus. There were about a hundred men and boys besides 15 or 20 women and children. As we drove up to the house, they retired at a respectable distance while we alighted. We were so tired that little or no enthusiasm was manifested on our part. But the sincere regard and respect of the group of men standing about was told in silence more than by words.
>
> Jesus, the faithful cook, was the embodiment of excitement; as he met his master, he wept big tears and embraced and kissed him over and over again. "This," I said to myself, "is something new to see a man kiss a man."

The group that greeted them included Nichols, Easterbrook, Thomason, Coffey, and Fred Staples.

Early in March of 1851, according to Mary Staples, Phoebe Ayer and her daughter ended their two-months stay at the ranch, and went to join Milo Ayer in Downieville. They were accompanied by Daniel Easterbrook. Milo Ayer had purchased a piece of mining property at Downieville, where he had built a home for his family, and to save time he remained in Sacramento to pack a string of mules with equipment for his project. His household goods were on the same boat that was bringing furniture for the Staples family. It is not known whether Phoebe and her child made the journey of nearly a hundred and fifty miles by stage or on muleback.

At that time there were few settlers in the vicinity of the Staples Ranch, and after Phoebe Ayer left for her own home, Mary Staples did not see another white woman for fully five months. She soon discovered, however, that the ranch was a sort of unofficial hotel, and hardly a day went by that at least one guest was not stopping with them, particularly after the stage coach began to operate between Stockton and Sacramento in July, 1851. The log house became a post office in September, 1851, and David was made postmaster of Staples Ranch, California. Earlier in the year he had been appointed justice of the peace of Elliott Township.

Staples was one of the organizers of the California Agricultural Society, in which he held a life membership, also serving as vice president for many years. The first wheat crop he sowed in early 1852 produced not only an excellent grade of grain but also a very heavy yield. It sold for 12½ cents per pound and was the first wheat produced in San Joaquin County that was used for seed. In another five years he owned more than one hundred acres of wheat, forty horses and mules, four yoke of oxen, thirty-five milk cows, one hundred hogs, and a big herd of beef cattle.

Staples' success in farming was a handy stepping stone to recognition in the community. In 1852, along with Dr. Dean Locke and others, he organized the Republican party in San Joaquin County, and in 1856 with Locke and another neighbor he called the county's first Republican convention. In 1860, Staples was chosen as a delegate to the Republican Presidential Convention in Chicago, where he cast his vote for Abraham Lincoln. The following year he traveled by stagecoach, steamboat, and train to Washington, D.C., to attend Lincoln's inauguration. He arrived too late for the ceremony, but just in time to enlist in the Cassius M. Clay Battalion, an organization of riflemen who, when a Confederate attack was feared, guarded the capital until regular army troops arrived and took over. The battalion was made up of men from all parts of the Union who had come to Washington on business, and Staples held the rank of captain.

In 1862, Leland Stanford, the newly elected governor of California, appointed Staples port warden of San Francisco. At this time the Staples Ranch was sold, and the family moved to a new home on Taylor Street in San Francisco. By this time there were three children; one daughter had died in infancy and a daughter was born in San Francisco. In 1866 Staples became vice president of the Fireman's Fund Insurance Company, and was elected president the following year, holding office for thirty-two years, until December 31, 1899. He was active in many civic and state organizations, and served as vice president of the Society of California Pioneers. It was one of his proudest accomplishments that he persuaded the financier James Lick to build the Lick Observatory at Mount Hamilton, California, instead of putting up a monument to himself.

Ill health eventually forced Staples' resignation from the Fireman's Fund Insurance Company, and the news brought a flood of letters and telegrams pouring onto his desk from all over the country. When he was in his seventies Staples wrote: "Next to being with my family [by which he meant his daughter and grandchildren; his wife had died in 1895], I like nothing better than to get out in the open next to nature." In fact, it was while on a camping trip that he caught a cold which turned into pneumonia and led to his death.

On April 3, 1900, the flags hung at half-mast throughout the city of San Francisco. What finer eulogy could any man hope for than the one David J. Staples received in the press that day: "He leaves as friends all who knew him, and a name that will find its place in the early history of the state."

MILO J. AYER
(See also under *David Staples*.) At Sutter's Fort, Ayer presumably found a letter from his cousin, Dr. Washington Ayer, who had

come west via Cape Horn. At any rate, the two cousins accompanied the group from the Boston-Newton company which eventually wound up mining in the Mokelumne Hill area, and at Rich Gulch Ayer's mining venture paid off.

In the latter part of 1850 he bought mining property near Downieville, and later developed several mines on this property. He built a house there and was joined by his wife and daughter, Belle, in March, 1851. The following year friends of the family came to California bringing with them the Ayer's young son, who had been left with relatives in Newton, Massachusetts. Tragically, a few days after his arrival the boy fell down a mine shaft and was killed.

In 1866 the family moved to Vallejo, where they built a country home in the hills just east of the town. Ayer was in the construction business, and is credited with building the first stamp mill in the California gold fields. Death came to this kindly and industrious man in 1900.

BENJAMIN BURT, JR.

Benjamin Burt began mining along the American River, being joined in the fall of 1850 by his brother, Simeon. He also kept a trading post where he bought and sold gold. In the early 1850's, he purchased eighty-five acres of tillable soil along Rancherio Creek, near Drytown and Plymouth. Here he built a cabin and sent east for fruit cuttings. In time he developed a fine orchard.

In 1855 he went back to Freetown, Massachusetts, where he married Orilla Jones, a schoolmate. The couple returned to California in July, and lived in the cabin while a fine new house was being built. After his ranch began producing, he freighted produce to Sacramento once a week and brought back provisions for his store. Burt held firmly to his conviction that carrying a gun only invites trouble, and though at this time express companies were preyed on by bandits, Burt had a record of no holdups. The Adams Express Company (later Wells Fargo) sought help from him, and for a number of years his wagon carried bags of gold dust concealed under a pile of fruit and vegetables.

The Burts had four daughters. When the younger children were ready for secondary school, Burt sold his ranch and trading post and the family moved to San Jose, where the California State Normal School was located. Daughters of the Staples and Locke families also were attending this school. It was in San Jose in 1896 that Benjamin Burt and his wife—two of the pioneers who had helped to build California—passed away, a week apart.

ROBERT COFFEY

(See also under *David Staples*.) Robert Coffey struck it rich at Goodyear's Bar near Downieville. When he was not in the mines with his brother John, he made his headquarters at the Staples Ranch, along with Easterbrook, Ayer, Nichols, Thomason, and Fred Staples during the first year or so after they arrived in California. All were registered there in 1852, when the Staples Ranch started out as a joint investment.

In 1853 Coffey bought two hundred and forty acres of land in Elkhorn Township, San Joaquin County, not far from the Staples Ranch. He was as successful in farming as in mining. He also bought and sold cattle, and later established business interests in Southern California, where he spent considerable time. Coffey, who is believed to have remained a bachelor, built a fine brick house and very substantial farm buildings on his ranch. Many acres of the farm were given over to an orchard. When the ranch was sold in 1890, he moved to San Francisco and was registered as living in the 700-block on Divisidero Street. He was sixty-eight at this time. There is no record of his death, so apparently he died before the 1906 earthquake and fire in which all records were lost.

HARVEY DICKINSON

Dickinson settled north of San Francisco. He served as a foreman of grand jury in San Francisco, and at a pioneer reunion there in 1880 is listed with a group of Forty Niners.

209

DANIEL E. EASTERBROOK

(See also under *David Staples.*) The youngest member of the Boston-Newton party became a capitalist at an early age. Whereever he put his spade in the ground, he always seemed to find gold. He struck it extra rich at Downieville in 1850, and from then on his fortune pyramided. People who were close to him say that some of his success came from his holding on to all of his claims, many of which continued to pay dividends years after the mining boom was over.

While he was at Downieville, Easterbrook had his finger in various ventures; in 1862 he owned a large livery stable there. Then, in 1866, he moved to Vallejo and some years later married Nettie Stone. For the next eighteen years they traveled abroad, and Easterbrook became well known for his art collection. Eventually he and his wife settled in Hayward, California, where they participated in the community projects and social life of the Bay area. (Curiously enough, Mrs. Easterbrook avoided references to her husband's pioneer day and preferred to stress his blue-blooded English ancestry.) The Easterbrooks had no children.

Easterbrook invested in many Bay area enterprises, and they continued to flourish. In fact, in 1949, a century after his arrival in California, his name was still on a San Francisco building. He died May 22, 1911, at Oakland. In his will he left a fund for scholarships at the University of California, as well as bequests to various institutions and organizations.

BENJAMIN EVANS
No information.

WALTON CHEEVER FELCH

(See also under *Charles Gould.*) After digging for gold on the American River for a year with Gould and Wilson, Felch decided to quit the mining fields and make use of his artistic talents. He opened an ornamental paint and sign shop on Fifth Street, between J and K Streets, in Sacramento. By this time his wife had come to California, and they settled down in a new house on

Tenth Street. He was a member of the volunteer fire department, and when the alarm sounded Felch would rush to put on his red jacket, grab the wooden bucket which bore his name, and make a dash for the firehouse. In later years, he went into the insurance business. He died in 1892.

James A. Hough
No information.

Dean Jewett Locke
(See also under *David Staples.*) In January, 1850, Dr. Locke began his mining career on the North Fork of the American River, thirty miles from Sacramento, where several of his trail companions already were operating. Some months later, because of the great demand for doctors, he returned to Sacramento, bought a lot on L Street, built a cabin, and hung out his sign. Subsequently, he went on to Mississippi Bar, where he mined, practiced medicine, and established a trading post.

In January, 1851, with his brother Elmer, he purchased three hundred and twenty acres of the Staples Ranch, and by April of that year the farm was well on its way, with a cabin and storehouse completed, a vegetable garden planted, a berry patch started, and grain fields ploughed. During the summer and fall Dr. Locke prospected in the Downieville area where several of the Boston-Newton group were having good luck in the gold fields.

In 1852 another brother, George, came out from Massachusetts to help supervise farming activities, and by 1853 the Locke Ranch began to show a healthy profit. In this year additional acreage was added, more land was put under cultivation, and horses and cattle began to fill the corrals. In 1854, Locke returned to his native Massachusetts and in the spring of 1855 married Delia Marcella Hammond of North Abington. They began the trip back to California in June of that year. By 1865 the Locke Ranch had mushroomed to more than a thousand acres, and the Lockes were the parents of five youngsters. Eventually they had thirteen children.

From the first Dr. Locke had been a leader in community activities—with David Staples he had organized the Republican party in the county, and had donated a large tract of land for the district school. After his return from the East he continued to launch one enterprise after another. Foremost among them was the establishing of a town—to which his wife gave the name of Lockeford—on his property. The first building in "his town" housed a general merchandise store and the post office, moved from Staples Ranch to Lockeford in 1862. Along with all his other activities, Dr. Locke continued to practice medicine. During his first years on the ranch he rode horseback on all calls; after roads were laid out in the new community he often rode in a gig—a light, two-wheeled cart—shipped from Massachusetts.

In 1866, when he was sixty-three, Dr. Locke was seriously injured in an accident, and was never able to carry on his work as before. Scarcely a year later he was stricken with pneumonia and died within a few days. One hundred and sixty carriages of friends and neighbors followed him to his last resting place on the Locke Ranch.

Brackett Lord

After mining near Downieville, Brackett Lord returned to Massachusetts in 1851. At this time, he and his wife had a daughter, Clarissa, and a son, John, and subsequently three children were born to them: Charles, Theodore, and Mary. A few years after his return to Massachusetts the rich land that Lord had seen in the Midwest on his trip to California drew him away from the Atlantic Coast. He settled in Edgar County, Illinois, and engaged in the buying and selling of grain and flour. He owned a large warehouse in Kansas, Illinois, and had grain interests in the nearby town of Paris. At one time he was the largest dealer in wheat in the Midwest. About 1867 he turned his business over to his eldest son, John Brackett Lord, and returned to Newton, Massachusetts, shortly before his death on June 25, 1872.

Nathaniel B. Loring

As reported in Chapter 12, Loring died in 1849 at Mokelumne Hill, of pneumonia contracted while he was taking care of Dr. Locke. It is pleasant to record that Dr. Locke allocated to Loring's widow a share equal to his own in a gold mine in the Downieville area.

Thomas H. McGrath

McGrath mined in the same part of the Feather River region as did James Wilson and Charles Gould. He was still a California resident in 1852,[1] but Wilson mentioned in a letter to Gould that McGrath returned to Massachusetts in 1857.

William H. Nichols

(See also under *David Staples*.) Nichols, a bachelor, shared the pioneer experiences of the Staples family in San Joaquin County. He and Staples were partners in the ranch from 1851 until it was sold in 1862. He then acquired a small tract of land and built a small house on it near the Locke home. When he became ill in 1879, Dr. Locke took Nichols into his home and cared for him until the end came. He was buried beside George Thomason in the Lockeford Cemetery.

Harry Noyes

As previously noted, no definite information is available on Harry Noyes. However, the late Helen Gould Trowbridge of Newton-ville, Massachusetts, recalled from her young days an elderly man of that name whose funeral was attended by several members of the Gould families in the Newton area. Similarly, when his son and daughter died the Goulds were represented at their funerals. Mrs. Trowbridge was convinced that the Harry Noyes she remembered was a member of the Boston-Newton company and that the friendship between the Noyes and Gould families was sealed during the days of the gold rush.

---

[1] There was another Thomas H. McGrath in the same area; he came to California in 1852 from Ireland.

S. D. OSBORN

No information. Only his initials are given on the roster that Robert Coffey prepared for Delia Locke in 1887 and on the one drawn up by Staples.

JOHN FREDERICK STAPLES

(See also under *David Staples.*) Soon after the Staples Ranch was bought, Fred Staples went into the cattle business on a large scale, using the ranch as his headquarters. He had business interests in Southern California, and after the ranch was sold settled in Pasadena with his family. Apparently he outlived his brother, for shortly before David Staples died he mentioned that his brother Fred was hale and hearty, well to do, and very generous to less fortunate people.

ALBION C. SWEETZER

(See also under *Charles Gould.*) As previously noted, Sweetzer, along with Felch, Wilson, Gould, and one other member of the Boston-Newton company (name not mentioned; probably McGrath) went to the North Fork of the American River when the company disbanded at Sutter's Fort. When the group found a location that suited them and began to build a log cabin that would serve both as living quarters and a store, Sweetzer went back to Sacramento and bought a load of supplies for the business venture. On his return trip to the mines a heavy rain made the roads almost impassable and his rented wagon was mired down several times before he reached the new cabin site. That was enough for Albion Sweetzer. He turned around and went back to Sacramento and never got any closer to the mines.

In Sacramento he went into the contracting business, and also entered the real estate and insurance fields. In 1850 he was prominent on the committee which arranged for the first Fourth of July celebration in Sacramento, and that same summer he organized a temperance society.

On December 12, 1853, Sweetzer was married to Sarah Pratt of Cambridge, Massachusetts. She had traveled by train and steamboat to Independence, and had crossed from there to Sacramento by covered wagon. Their only child died in 1857. In later years the Sweetzers' home became a gathering place for members of the Boston-Newton company, who congregated there when they were in Sacramento and spent many an hour talking about the days of '49. Sweetzer prospered in his business and was active in community affairs, serving as a member of the board of education as well as holding various other civic posts. So far as is known, he attained the most advanced age of any of the Boston-Newton party. He died in 1910, when he was ninety-one.

GEORGE THOMASON
(See also under *David Staples*.) After Thomason gave up mining, he bought land adjacent to the town of Lockeford and started a farm. At that time his wife, Mercy, came to California from Massachusetts. However, she regarded New England as her real home, and she left her husband and returned to Massachusetts after the death of their infant son in 1856. Thomason became ill in 1873 and was cared for until his death by Dean Locke and William Nichols. He was buried beside his son's grave in the Lockeford Cemetery. Three links of a chain—the symbol of his lodge, the Independent Order of Odd Fellows—decorate the marker. The cemetery was a part of the Staples Ranch deeded by David Staples to the community in 1859 for "a church, a rectory and a cemetery." Staples, who also was a member of the I.O.O.F., stipulated there be free burial for all lodge members.

JOHN WHITE
At the reunion of the Society of California Pioneers in 1880, John White signed the register. He was a resident of San Francisco.

LEWIS K. WHITTIER
In 1850 and 1851 Whittier was a police officer in Sacramento. He was twenty-eight years old at this time.

JAMES ST. CLAIRE WILSON
(See also under *Charles Gould.*) After beginning his mining career in 1849 on the North Fork of the American River with four of his trail companions, Wilson and Gould explored the mining region farther north and west of their first location the following summer. In the fall of 1950 Wilson returned to Massachusetts via Panama, and came back to California within a few months, bringing his wife, Mary, a son, five, and a daughter, three. Their first home was at Wyman Ravine, Butte County, where they were living in 1854. For a number of years the children attended the Pratt School in Sacramento, living there during the school term.

In 1862 James Wilson was in the office of the treasurer of Sierra Nevada County, and apparently living in Downieville. In a letter written to Gould that year he said that his wife was seriously ill; that his oldest son was seventeen; and that he had three daughters. In addition to discussing land prices and routes to California, he wrote: "Two of our old co. are here Easterbrook and Ayers. E. is rich. Felch and Sweetzer are in Sacramento, I see them every three months. Dave Staples has the appointment of Port Warden of San Francisco." He also referred to Wyman Ravine, American Valley, and Oroville, "our old Ophir." This is the last information found on James Wilson.

GEORGE WINSLOW
In the summer of 1911, George Hansen, a Fairbury, Nebraska, banker, representing the Nebraska State Historical Society, journeyed to Massachusetts and Connecticut to visit George Winslow's sons. He told them that he had seen their father's grave and that "the inscription on the stone was as distinct as though freshly cut." Hansen had been able to locate copies of two letters written on the trail: one by George Winslow sent from Independence and the other by Brackett Lord written at the side of Winslow's grave and mailed at Fort Kearny. (The letters appear in Chapter 6.) A daughter of Lord lived near the Winslows in Connecticut, and

it was from her that he had obtained a copy of the Brackett Lord letter. Hansen learned from the Winslows that Charles Gould had kept a diary of the 1849 journey, and that he lived at Lake City, Minnesota.

While Hansen was in the East, arrangements were made by the Nebraska Historical Society and the Winslow families to put up the large monument which now marks the burial place of George Winslow. The granite slab came from the Winslow farm in Connecticut, and the plaque was made[2] by Winslow's younger son, Henry, who had been born on the day that the Boston-Newton company camped at Blue Prairie. The plaque reads:

In memory of
George Winslow
who died on this great highway
June 8 1849 and was buried here
by his comrades of the Boston and
Newton Joint Stock Association
this tablet is affectionately placed
by his sons
George Edward
and
Orin Henry Winslow

Embedded in the granite slab beneath the plaque is the original marker put up by the Boston-Newton company.

JESSE WINSLOW

Jesse Winslow remained in the mines two years before returning to Massachusetts. Before his departure he visited his niece, Mary Staples Winslow, and later presented her with a set of jewelry made from gold which he had mined. He died in 1872 at the age of seventy-eight.

---

[2] The Winslow Company made plaques as well as silverware, etc. In 1950 the Winslow name was still on the company's building in Meriden, Connecticut. The firm is now known as the International Silver Company.

217

A NOTE ON SOURCES

Tracking down information about the members of the Boston-Newton company has occupied me on and off over a long period of time, although my most intensive work was undertaken over the period of a year at the Bancroft Library. I also spent two months in the Boston area, working in the Houghton and Baker Libraries at Harvard, at the library of the Massachusetts Institute of Technology, and at the Boston Public Library. In addition, I have corresponded with many historical societies and other archives, as the list of acknowledgments indicates. My purpose in this note is to indicate the main sources of my information about Charles Gould and David Staples and other members of the company. Full bibliographical information for printed sources referred to in the text is given in the footnotes. Printed and manuscript materials were supplemented by letters from, and conversations with, the descendants of the men of the Boston-Newton company whose names appear in the Acknowledgments.

Charles Gould

Two journals, "Across the Plains 1849" and "Via the Isthmus Route 1852," at the Minnesota Historical Society. Diary of Major John Allen Gould, now in the possession of Gardner Gould, Newtonville, Massachusetts. Letters from James St. Claire Wilson dated 1854, June 8, 1857, and March 29, 1862, now in the possession of the Rossman family, Grand Rapids, Minnesota. Passport, March 24, 1849, #1628, Archives Division, Office of the Secretary, The Commonwealth of Massachusetts, Boston.

David J. Staples

Journal at the Bancroft Library, University of California, Berkeley. Published as "The Journal of David Jackson Staples," edited by Harold F. Taggart, *California Historical Society Quarterly*, XXII (June, 1943), 119–150. The Staples Papers, 1849–1900, C-D 158, C-D 288, C-D 289.1, at the Bancroft Library. Details of Staples' boyhood are given in C-D 288. Included in these papers are an account of the trip west written by Staples for the Bancroft Library; Memoirs, 1852–1870, by Mary Winslow Staples; scrapbook belonging to Mary Winslow Staples which includes published articles written by her and newspaper clippings about family happenings. Roster of the Boston-Newton company prepared in 1891 by Staples. Passport, March 22, 1849, #1624, Archives Division, Commonwealth of Massachusetts, Boston. *The Winslow Memorial*, edited by David Parsons Holton and Frances K. Holton (New York, 1877), I, 469, 470–471. *A Romance of Insurance*, by Frank Morton Todd (San Francisco: Fireman's Fund Insurance Co., 1929). *Still Flying and Nailed to the Mast*, by William Bronson (Garden City, N.Y.: Doubleday, 1963).

Milo J. Ayer

Records of the Society of California Pioneers. David and Mary Staples Papers. Staples Roster, 1891. Reports from members of the Ayer family. Letter from Wilson to Gould, March 29, 1862.

Benjamin Burt

The Winslow Memorial, I, 460. Clara Burt Journal, 1870–1900, at the Bancroft Library (includes newspaper clippings). Staples Roster, 1891. Reports from descendants.

Robert Coffey

Census records. Clara Burt Journal. Delia Locke Journal, Vol. I (see below). The Staples Papers. Staples Roster, 1891.

Harvey W. Dickinson

Census records. Pioneer Reunion, San Francisco, 1880. Staples Roster, 1891.

Daniel E. Easterbrook

Information at the California State Historical Society. Report from the Ayer family. Death notice, May 22, 1911. Letter from Wilson to Gould, 1862. Staples Roster, 1891.

Benjamin C. Evans

Staples Roster, 1891.

Walton C. Felch

Passport, April 2, 1849, #1719, Archives Division, Commonwealth of Massachusetts. Staples Roster, 1891.

James A. Hough

Passport, March 22, 1849, #1625, Archives Division, Commonwealth of Massachusetts. Staples Roster, 1891.

Dean Jewett Locke

Journal, "California Mines 1850–1852," in the possession of Theresa Locke Thorp, Lockeford, California. Journal by Delia Locke, "Life at Lockeford, California, 1855–1918," 14 vols., in the possession of Theresa Locke Thorp. Passport, April 10, 1849, #1730, Archives Division, Commonwealth of Massachusetts. Reports from Dr. Locke's children.

Brackett Lord

The Winslow Memorial, I, 465. *Nebraska State Historical Society Collections,* XVII, 124–126. File of prominent Illinois citizens, Chicago City Library. Reports from Lord family. Staples Roster, 1891.

Nathaniel Loring

Passport, March 2, 1849, #1718, Archives Division, Commonwealth of Massachusetts. Vital records, Newton, Massachusetts. Dean Jewett Locke Journal. Reports from Loring family. Staples Roster, 1891.

Thomas H. McGrath
Staples Roster, 1891. Letter from Wilson to Gould, June 8, 1857.

William H. Nichols
Passport, March 24, 1849, #1629, in the possession of Edna Locke Pierce, Lockeford, California. The Staples Papers. Delia Locke Journal. Staples Roster, 1891. County records in the George Thomason estate. Lockeford Cemetery. Reports from the late Hannah Locke Demangeot and Edward Locke.

Harry Noyes
Staples Roster, 1891. Information from Helen Gould Trowbridge, Newtonville, Massachusetts.

S. D. Osborn
Staples Roster, 1891.

John Frederick Staples
The Staples Papers. Staples Roster, 1891.

Albion C. Sweetzer
Passport, April 2, 1849, #1714, Archives Division, Commonwealth of Massachusetts. *History of Sacramento County* (Oakland: Thompson & West, 1880), p. 292. W. J. Davis, *Illustrated History of Sacramento County* (Chicago: Lewis Publishing Co., 1890), pp. 566–567. Sacramento *Bee*, August 30, 1910, 5:3. San Francisco *Call*, August 31, 1910, 7:7. Biographical card, California State Library, Sacramento. Staples Roster, 1891.

George Thomason
Staples Roster, 1891. Delia Locke Journal. Lockeford Cemetery. County records. Letter from Mrs. Scott Rountree, Piedmont, California.

John White
Staples Roster, 1891. Pioneer Reunion, San Francisco, 1880.

Lewis K. Whittier
> Staples Roster, 1891. Census record.

James St. Claire Wilson
> Passport, April 2, 1849, #1713. Letters to Gould, 1854, 1857,
> 1862. Staples Roster, 1891.

George Winslow
> Letter to Eliza Winslow, May, 1849, at the Nebraska State
> Historical Society, Lincoln, Nebraska. Published in George
> W. Hansen, "A Tragedy of the Oregon Trail," *Nebraska
> State Historical Society Collections*, XVII (1913), 110–126.
> *The Winslow Memorial*, I, 468. Staples Roster, 1891.

Jesse Winslow
> *The Winslow Memorial*, I, 463. Record of vital statistics,
> Newton, Massachusetts. Staples Roster, 1891. The Staples
> Papers.

Other manuscript sources not listed elsewhere include:
> Edwin Wilson. "Lake City, Minnesota, 1860–1914." In the
> possession of Lillian Wilson Strand, Centerville, South
> Dakota.
> Rev. James Woods. "Recollections of Pioneer Life in Cali-
> fornia, 1849–1878." Manuscript. At the Felton Library,
> Felton, California.

Newspapers and periodicals not listed elsewhere include:
> (In California) *Daily Californian* (Berkeley); *Gazette*
> (Berkeley); San Francisco *Chronicle*; *Mountain Democrat*
> (Placerville); *Times* (Placerville). Also, Lake City, Min-
> nesota, *Republican*; Fairbury, Nebraska, *News*; *Nebraska
> State Journal*; *Waterways Journal* (St. Louis, Missouri);
> *Newton Progress* (Newton, Massachusetts).

ACKNOWLEDGMENTS

The author wishes to express her appreciation to the following archives and organizations for their generous assistance during the preparation of this book:

(In California) The Society of California Pioneers, San Francisco; the California Historical Society, San Francisco; the Bancroft Library, University of California, Berkeley; the Berkeley Public Library; the Henry E. Huntington Library and Art Gallery, San Marino; the State Library, Sacramento; the Los Angeles Public Library; the Monrovia Public Library; the Kern County Historical Society, Bakersfield; the Haggin Memorial Galleries and Pioneer Museum, Stockton; the California State Chamber of Commerce, San Francisco; the El Dorado County Chamber of Commerce, Placerville; and the Fireman's Fund Insurance Company of San Francisco.

(In Massachusetts) The Houghton and Baker Libraries, Harvard University, Cambridge; the Massachusetts Institute of Technology Library, Cambridge; the Boston Public Library; the Antiquarian Public Library, Worcester; the Newton Chamber of Commerce, Newton.

Also to the Yale University Library, New Haven, Connecticut; the Newberry Library, Chicago, Illinois; the Chicago Public Library; the Saline County Historical Museum, Salina, Kansas; the J. B. Speed Art Museum, Louisville, Kentucky; the Louisville Chamber of Commerce; the Minnesota Historical Society, St. Paul; the Hermann Chamber of Commerce, Hermann, Missouri; the Nebraska State Historical Society, Lincoln, Nebraska; the Fairbury Chamber of Commerce, Fairbury, Nebraska; the Buffalo Historical Society, Buffalo, New York; The Historical and Philosophical Society of Ohio, Cincinnati, Ohio; the Cincinnati Public Library; the Utah Historical Society, Salt Lake City, Utah; The Mariner's Museum, Newport News, Virginia; and in Washington, D.C., the National Archives, the Smithsonian Institution Library, and the Library of Congress.

For the helpful information and interesting sidelights they graciously provided, the author is indebted to a long list of persons, many of them descendants of the members of the Boston-Newton Joint Stock Association. Her special thanks go to Gardner Gould of Newton, Massachusetts; Theresa Locke Thorpe, Neil H. Locke, Don and Donna Locke, and Edna Locke Pierce, all of Lockeford, California; also to Ray F. Herrod and to Clyde and Marcia Engle, Oakland, California; to Milo J. Ayer, Berkeley; to Bess Painter, San Mateo, California; to David Winslow, San Francisco; and to Edward S. Clark, Felton, California. Regrettably, a number of descendants who merit the author's gratitude have passed on, among them Helen Gould Trowbridge and Margaret Gould Lemmon; David Staples Painter; Hannah Locke Demangoet, Edward M. Locke, and Dr. George H. Locke; Burt Herrod; Mabel Mayon; Howard S. Engle; Evelyn Clark; Lawrence A. Rossman and Willard Rossman.

This list would be incomplete without mention of the following people who were of invaluable assistance: Dr. George P. Hammond, Robert W. Parkinson, and Robert and Alice LaMotte of Berkeley; Harold F. Taggart, San Mateo; Helen S. Giffen, Society of California Pioneers, San Francisco; the Honorable Joseph R. Knowland and Jane Voiles, Oakland; Kenneth M. Brown, Palo Alto, Theodore Baggelmann, Sacramento; Alex and Anita Andres, Shingle Springs, California; Glenn R. Leroy, Fairbury, Nebraska; and Frederick Way, Jr., Sewickly, Pennsylvania.